(690 · 12 BIC)

TCl

PARTY WALLS
THE NEW LAW

PARTY WALLS
THE NEW LAW

Stephen Bickford-Smith BA, FCIArb,
Barrister and Registered Arbitrator,
Master of the Bench of the Inner Temple

and

Colin Sydenham MA
Barrister

both of 4 Breams Buildings, London

JORDANS
1997

Published by
Jordan Publishing Limited
21 St Thomas Street
Bristol BS1 6JS

British Library Cataloguing-in-Publication Data
A catalogue record for this book is available from the British Library.

ISBN 0 85308 401 7

Typeset by Mendip Communications Ltd, Frome, Somerset
Printed in Great Britain by Biddles Ltd, Guildford and King's Lynn

FOREWORD

The traditional role of the parliamentarian is to be a competent generalist not a specialist and this time-honoured dictum is surely more appropriate today than ever. The conflicting public interest agendas facing Parliament certainly make for a difficult balancing act. The power of the consumer and the UK property market as a whole present special challenges to anyone attempting to change the law not least because of the potential for conflict over important legal principles.

So I was both delighted and challenged to be asked to sponsor a Party Wall Bill in the Upper House and to have the experience of taking a Parliamentary Bill through all its stages. But it was very much a team effort with professionals of many disciplines having an input of immense value. If I came into the arena of party wall legislation by chance, the request to write this Foreword was less accidental, via Colin Sydenham's wife, Angela, whom I have known for several years as the Chief Legal Adviser of the Country Landowners Association. There have been other happy associations with the Chambers at 4 Breams Buildings so it is an enormous pleasure to return the compliment and to say how pleased I am as a mere chartered surveyor to have a slot at the beginning of a book written by two of the leading experts in this field. I am especially glad to have had the draft text from Stephen Bickford-Smith and to note the skill with which the co-authors have woven together the old and the new legislation via the parliamentary procedure and the unique insight it gives into that process.

High on the national agenda is the whole question of neighbour and consumer disputes; the perception that they take too long to resolve, that they are too costly and that they impede economic efficiency has fuelled much debate. Belloc, in writing some witty epigrams to my great grandfather, ends one ribald assault on an adversary with the words 'never mind the where and how, only – let him have it now!'. Disputes should be resolved efficiently and it is for this that the party wall procedures are rightly praised. For generations, property owners in inner London have settled their differences without going to court. The fact that there have been so few appeals from party wall awards is testimony in itself but beyond that lies a model dispute resolution structure that is tested and sophisticated. In modern environmental parlance, it ensures that the circumstances of a dispute are 'internalised'.

As this book shows so concisely, the procedures of party walls can be both simple and complex but complexity carries with it a price tag which can be directly related to the cost-benefit of a course of action *before* it is irrevocably undertaken. There is no ransom situation or right of absolute veto as happens in some other areas and the procedures are not court-driven. I hope that this philosophy may in due course be applied more widely.

The Earl of Lytton
Newbuildings Place, Horsham
October 1996

PREFACE

'Nam tua res agitur paries cum proximus ardet.'
(For it is your business if your neighbour's party wall catches fire.)
(Horace Epistles I, xviii, 84)

The words of Horace attest the antiquity of concerns about party walls. And no wonder, since man is an intensely territorial animal, and party walls demarcate the boundaries between adjoining private territories. Two millennia after Horace, Robert Frost's neighbour observed that 'Good fences make good neighbours', yet the common law, with its insistence on the sanctity of each neighbour's property rights, will often frustrate the good neighbour who wishes to repair, rebuild or improve (let alone develop) a party wall.

As a result, local statutory regimes have been enacted which establish summary procedures enabling party walls to be dealt with in ways which are approved by a panel of surveyors. The best known of these regimes is in Inner London, where its origins can be traced back to the years immediately after the Great Fire. A succession of London Building Acts culminated in that of 1939, which still owed much to its predecessor of 1894. Now, for the first time, this metropolitan regime, with relatively minor modifications, is to be extended to the whole of England and Wales by the Party Wall etc Act 1996.

The relaxation of the common law straitjacket is welcome. So is the unique and expeditious procedure for the resolution of disputes. The system has worked well in London, and this is demonstrated by the fact that only a handful of cases on it have reached the law reports this century. Partly this success must be attributable to a corps of experienced surveyors who are familiar with the legislation: partly also, no doubt, to ignorance of the legislation on the part of the public, coupled with neighbourly forbearance.

Whether the system will work well on a countrywide scale remains to be seen. The Law Society opposed the Bill, partly on the ground that the costs of the dispute resolution procedure will be out of proportion to the modest value of many of the properties which will now be affected. There are technical reservations too. The Act is by no means emancipated from its nineteenth century parentage. It imposes contingent liabilities on owners of land, but it is a stranger to the techniques of registration which have been with us since 1925. It does not recognise the existence of successors in title. It is harsh to occupiers who do not satisfy its definition of 'owner'. These points are elaborated in the text.

Halsbury apart, there is no book on party walls written by and for practising lawyers, and there are many professionals throughout the country, surveyors and land agents as well as lawyers, who will now need to familiarise themselves with the workings of the 1996 Act. This book is intended for them. We have endeavoured not only to provide an introduction to the Act, but to set the legislation in its conveyancing and property law context. The appendices include the text of the 1996 Act and of Part VI of the 1939 Act, a checklist of the notices that are required by the 1996 Act, and a set of precedents. We hope that these will all be of practical use. We have not thought it necessary to include the text of the 1894 Act, but in preparing this book we have had frequent recourse to the commentary on that Act written by A.R. Rudall and published, as it happens, by Jordan & Sons Ltd in 1922. It is appropriate that this book should be published under the successor imprint. We record our grateful thanks to the professional team who have helped us through the pains of authorship. The authors and publishers are grateful to The Stationery Office for giving their kind permission to reproduce the statutory materials in this book.

STEPHEN BICKFORD-SMITH
COLIN SYDENHAM
December 1996

CONTENTS

TABLE OF CASES

References in the right-hand column are to paragraph numbers; references in *italics* are to page numbers.

TABLE OF STATUTES

References in the right-hand column are to paragraph numbers; references in *italics* are to page numbers. Page references printed in bold type indicate where an Act is set out in part or in full.

TABLE OF STATUTORY INSTRUMENTS

Chapter 1

INTRODUCTION TO THE ACT

1.1 ORIGIN OF THE ACT

The Party Wall etc Act 1996 received Royal Assent on 18th July 1996. By s 22(2) the Act comes into force in accordance with provision made by the Secretary of State for the Environment by Order made by Statutory Instrument. The Act was introduced as a Private Members Bill into the House of Lords by Lord Lytton, a practising chartered surveyor. Although a Private Members Bill, it received Government support. It completed its passage through the Lords on 22 May 1996, and passed all its stages in the Commons on 12 July 1996. It is referred to hereafter simply as 'the Act'.

1.2 ANTECEDENTS

After the fire of London in 1666, 'Commissioners for rebuilding' were appointed, on the basis of whose recommendations an Act for the rebuilding of London[1] was enacted. One of the primary purposes of that Act was to lay down requirements for new buildings to ensure that a general conflagration could not once again occur. Section 8 of the Act required:

> 'That there be party-walls and party-piers, set out equally on each building ground, to be built up by the first beginner of such building and that convenient toothing be left in the front wall by the said first builder, for the better joining of the next house that shall be built to the same: (2) and that no man may be permitted by the said surveyors, to build on the said party wall, or on his own contiguous ground, until he hath fully reimbursed the said first builder before full moiety of the charges of the said party-wall and pier ...'

The 1667 Act, which was limited in application to the City of London, made no provision for the demolition or alteration of party walls. Subsequent legislation in the eighteenth and nineteenth centuries elaborated the position. The culmination of two centuries of legislation, and the origin of the present law, is the London Building Act 1894. This was amended in 1905 and replaced in 1930 by the London Building Act 1930, a consolidating statute. The relevant law was subsequently re-embodied with amendments in Part VI of the London Building Acts (Amendment) Act 1939. By s 1 of that Act, it was to be read and construed as one with the 1930 Act. These Acts are hereafter referred to by date alone.

---

1 19 Car IIc.3.

1.3   THE 1939 ACT

In all its essentials, the Act repeats provisions already contained in the 1939 Act, the material text of which is set out in Appendix 2. The 1939 Act is a local Act, applying only to the Inner London Boroughs.[2] Although it is intended that the 1939 Act will be repealed once the Act comes into force, judicial decisions on its provisions and their predecessors will be of relevance in construing the corresponding provisions of the Act. In Parliament, it was stated that the purpose of the Act was to extend the 'tried and tested' provisions of the 1939 Act to the whole country,[3] and it is thought, therefore, that existing case-law on the previous legislation will continue to apply, except where a change in language compels a different conclusion.[4]

1.4   OPERATION OF THE ACT

Party walls separating the lands of adjoining owners are sensitive areas at common law. Since each owner has some interest in the wall, often neither can do any work to it without the consent of the other, which may lead to paralysis. The broad object of the Act is to set up machinery enabling the building owner to carry out works within the scope of the Act. The machinery starts with a notice under the Act, and, unless the adjoining owner consents, this sets in train an elaborate procedure for referring the matter to surveyors for determination. The surveyors embody their decision in an award which, subject to the possibility of appeal to the county court, is binding on both parties.

1.5   STRUCTURE OF THE BOOK

This book attempts to explain the detailed workings of the Act. Its structure is as follows.

1.5.1   Definitions

Chapter 2 introduces the basic concepts of the Act, defined in s 20 (party wall, building owner, adjoining owner etc).

1.5.2   Substantive rights

Chapter 3 describes the principal substantive rights conferred by the Act, namely:

---

2 See London Government Act 1963, s 43.

3 See Hansard HL Debates, Vol 568, 31 Jan 1996, Col 1536.

4 Compare *EWP Ltd v Moore* [1992] QB 460, CA. For the general approach where statutory provisions are the subject of decided cases having been repealed and re-enacted, see *R v Bow Road Domestic Proceedings Court ex parte Adedigba* [1968] 2 All ER 89.

(a) rights to build where the boundary is not already built on (s 1);

(b) rights to build where the boundary is already built on (s 2).

This requires an explanation of the notices which the building owner has to serve (under ss 1 and 3), and the adjoining owner's right to serve a counter-notice (s 4), and the way disputes are deemed to arise (s 5).

1.5.3 Adjacent excavation

The Act also applies where the building owner's operations on his own land involve excavating to defined depths within 3 or 6 metres of a building of the adjoining owner (s 6). This is dealt with in Chapter 4.

1.5.4 Special foundations

The Act makes some miscellaneous provisions about 'special foundations'. These are brought together in Chapter 5.

1.5.5 Ancillary rights and obligations

The Act creates a number of ancillary rights (eg to compensation for damage) and obligations (eg not to cause unnecessary inconvenience). These are found mainly in s 7, but also elsewhere. They are dealt with in Chapter 6, except for the important rights of entry for the purposes of the Act (s 8), which are separately dealt with in Chapter 7.

1.5.6 Award

Section 10 enacts the complex machinery for the appointment of the surveyors, and the determination of disputes by their award. This is separated into three chapters: Chapter 8 on Procedure and Scope; Chapter 9 on Effect and Enforcement; and Chapter 10 on Rights of Appeal.

1.5.7 Financial matters

In general, the building owner has to pay the expenses of the works, but there are a number of circumstances in which the adjoining owner has to contribute. The complex financial provisions of s 11 are dealt with in Chapter 11, which also covers the machinery for recovering costs from an adjoining owner (ss 13 and 14).

1.5.8 Security

Chapter 12 is concerned with s 12, which enables each party to claim security for expenses against the other.

1.5.9 Notices

There are many forms of notice which the Act requires to be served. These are referred to throughout the text. Precedents are provided in Appendix 4, and checklists in Appendix 3. Chapter 13 deals only with the methods of service prescribed by the Act (s 15).

1.5.10 Successors in title

Although the Act affects land, and creates contingent liabilities for owners of land, it makes no reference to successors in title. Chapter 14 tackles this difficulty, and includes a brief look at the conveyancing problems.

1.5.11 Other areas of law

Chapter 15 covers s 9, which preserves certain common law rights, and deals with the Act's relationship to other areas of law, including statute law.

1.5.12 Criminal offences

Finally, Chapter 16 deals with s 16, which creates criminal offences in connection with the rights of entry under s 8.

1.5.13 Appendices

Appendix 1 contains the text of the Act, with a brief commentary, and Appendix 5 lists the Hansard references to the Bill in both Houses of Parliament, since these are now admissible as an aid to construction.[5] The other three appendices have already been introduced.

1.6 APPLICATION

The Act binds land belonging to the Crown,[6] but land in Inner London belonging to the Inns of Court is excepted.[7]

1.7 COMMENCEMENT AND TRANSITIONAL PROVISIONS

Section 21 (1) gives the Secretary of State power to amend or repeal earlier local Acts. The intention is to exercise this power by repealing the 1939 Act when the

---

5 See *Pepper (Inspector of Taxes) v Hart* [1993] AC 593.

6 See s 19.

7 See s 18.

Act comes into force.[8] The order is expected to provide that the Act will come into force on 1 April 1997 and to contain transitional provisions which have the effect that:

(a) existing proceedings in Inner London under the 1939 Act are preserved;

(b) the time-limits for service of notices under the Act are adjusted to accommodate work in progress or programmed to start shortly after the Act comes into force.

At the time of going to press, the draft order was at consultative stage.

---

8 It is not intended, however, to repeal the local Acts containing provisions relating to party walls. These include the Middlesex County Council Act 1956, s 37; the Greater Manchester Act 1981, s 43; the Leicestershire County Council Act 1985, s 36; the Nottinghamshire County Council Act 1985, s 5; the West Glamorgan Act 1987, s 27; and the Bristol Improvement Act 1847, ss 24–32.

Chapter 2

APPLICATION OF THE ACT

2.1 DEFINITIONS

The terms of art defined by the Act are set out in s 20. It is necessary to start with an explanation of the basic concepts.

2.2 PARTY WALL

This is defined as follows:

> '(a) a wall which forms part of a building and stands on lands of different owners to a greater extent than the projection of any artificially formed support on which the wall rests; and
>
> (b) so much of a wall not being a wall referred to in paragraph (a) above as separates buildings belonging to different owners.'

It will be seen that all party walls are, in a broad sense, boundary walls, which belong to one or more buildings. Paragraph (a) is concerned with external walls of single buildings. The wall must stand astride the boundary, partly (not necessarily equally) in one property and partly in the other; if the whole of the wall is on one side of the boundary, and only its foundations or footings project into the other side, it is not a party wall. Paragraph (b) is concerned with walls attached to buildings on both sides (eg between terraced houses). These do not have to stand astride the boundary, and may be wholly on one side of it; what matters is that they separate buildings belonging to different owners. The effect of these two definitions is illustrated in Figure 1 below. Both paragraphs carry difficulties.

2.2.1 Overhangs

Paragraph (a) does not define the status of overhangs. A wall may be entirely on one side of the boundary at ground level, but be corbelled out at a higher level, so as to overhang the adjoining land. Can such a wall, or its thickened upper part, be said to 'stand on' lands of different owners? Can 'on' include 'over' in this context? Upon the ordinary use of language, it is thought the answer to both questions is no. And this conclusion seems to be supported by s 2(1)(h), which expressly contemplates overhangs. It may, nevertheless, be arguable that a wall of this kind is a party wall to the extent that it overhangs the adjoining land.

2.2.2 Trespassing buildings

Paragraph (b) gives rise to the question of the trespassing building. If a boundary wall is sited entirely on A's land, and B proceeds, without permission,

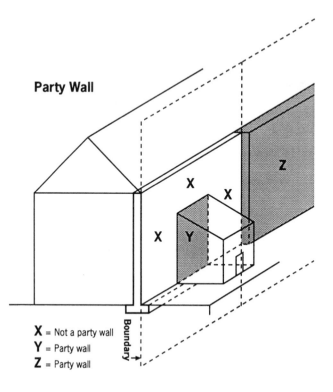

Party Wall

Z

X
X
X   Y

X = Not a party wall
Y = Party wall
Z = Party wall

Boundary

Figure 1

to construct a building against it, the wall becomes a paragraph (b) party wall so far as the building extends. Does this mean that B becomes immediately entitled to claim the rights conferred by the Act? And if not immediately, how soon? It is considered that the answers lie in the law of adverse possession. By enclosing on A's wall, B is not merely trespassing, he is taking possession of its surface, which is part of A's land. If B serves some notice claiming rights which the Act appears to give him, A can negate the notice by suing for removal of the trespassing building, and will be entitled to succeed unless B has acquired title by 12 years' adverse possession. If B wants immediate rights which will not be vulnerable to this response, he must negotiate with A for them: and if A wants to keep full control of his wall, he should grant no more than a revocable licence to attach the building, which will prevent B's possession being adverse.[1]

---

1 See *Heslop v Burns* [1974] 1 WLR 1241.

2.3 PARTY FENCE WALL

This is defined as:

> 'a wall (not being part of a building) which stands on lands of different owners and is used or constructed to be used for separating such adjoining lands, but does not include a wall constructed on the land of one owner the artificially formed support of which projects into the land of another owner.'

Like a paragraph (a) party wall, a party fence wall is a wall which stands astride the boundary between two properties and, if only its foundations or footings project beyond the boundary, it is disqualified in the same way. The distinction is that the party fence wall does not form part of a building; it is essentially free-standing (eg a garden wall). See Figure 2 below.

2.4 PARTY STRUCTURE

This is defined as:

> 'a party wall and also a floor partition or other structure separating buildings or parts of buildings approached solely by separate staircases or separate entrances.'

This translates the concept of party wall from the vertical dimension to the horizontal, and also to the microcosm of parts of buildings approached by separate staircases or entrances (eg flats). The confusing qualifying words 'from without' have been pruned from the 1939 definition, thus removing doubts about the application to flats. All floors, ceilings and walls separating adjoining flats are party structures.

2.5 OWNER

There is a threefold definition of 'owner' which can be summarised as including:

(a) anyone receiving, or entitled to receive, the rents and profits;

(b) anyone in possession (except a mortgagee, a tenant at will, or a periodic tenant from year to year or a lesser period);

(c) a contractual purchaser of an interest in the land, including a contract for a lease (other than a periodic tenancy of the kind excluded from (b)).

Authorities on the predecessors of this definition should be approached with caution, since they turn on different wording, and sometimes apply provisions which no longer appear in the Act.[2] Limb (a), it seems, does not include a

---

2 For example *Wigg v Lefevre* (1892) 8 TLR 493, holding that a lessee for 35 years, who had sub-let, was not an owner under the Metropolitan Building Act 1855, is no longer applicable.

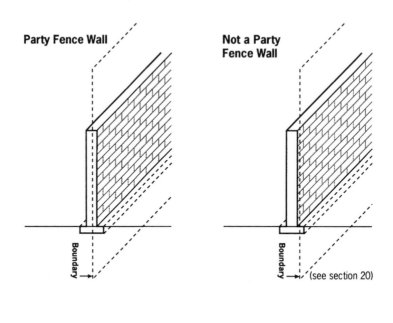

Figure 2

person, such as a receiver, who is in receipt of rent as agent for another.[3] Limb (c) is new. It gives the standing of owner to a purchaser of the freehold or who has a contract for the grant of a qualifying lease.[4] It does not appear to deprive a vendor of his standing under (a) or (b).

This definition controls the subsidiary definitions of **building owner**, which simply means an owner who wishes to exercise rights under the Act, and **adjoining owner** which means the owner of land, buildings, storeys or rooms adjoining that of the building owner. In this context, 'adjoining' appears to carry its strict meaning of 'contiguous', 'having physical contact', since it needs express extension to embrace owners within the distances defined by s 6 (see s 20).[5]

---

3 See *Solomons v R Gertzenstein Ltd* [1954] 2 All ER 625.

4 It is still not wide enough to include the plaintiff in *Spiers and Son Ltd v Troup* (1915) 84 LJKB 1986, who had not even exchanged contracts.

5 See *Re Ecclesiastical Commissioners for England's Conveyance* [1936] Ch 430. But if there are flat-owners who will be affected by works at a lower level, it might embrace them through its extended meaning of 'neighbouring': see *Cave v Horsell* [1912] 3 KB 533.

This concept of ownership is fundamental to the Act. It gives rights to building owners, which are controlled by competing rights which it gives to adjoining owners. But to adjoining occupiers who do not qualify as owners – and they include a large class of periodic tenants – it gives rights of compensation[6] and the right to receive notice before their property is entered,[7] but they have no right to be heard in the deliberations leading to the award which determines what works are to be carried out.

2.6 OTHER EXPRESSIONS

It is somewhat confusing to find that the Act employs a number of other expressions which, although they appear to be used in a technical way which does not command immediate comprehension, are nevertheless not supplied with definitions. Their meaning has to be deduced from their context.

2.6.1 Fence wall

This expression, which does not appear to have any ordinary meaning, is found in s 1(4)(b). It is used there to denote a wall which would be a party fence wall, if it was not built solely on the land of one owner, ie a free-standing boundary wall, not part of a building.

2.6.2 External wall

The normal meaning of this expression would be an outside wall, whether free-standing or part of a building. But in s 1(4)(b) it is used, in contra-distinction to 'fence wall', of a wall which would be a party wall if it was not built wholly on the land of one owner. This suggests that its meaning is restricted to the outside wall of a building. On the other hand, in s 2(1) the use of the expression 'external wall of a building' suggests the normal meaning. There are other contexts which provide no guidance (eg ss 2(2)(g) and (3)(b)). Section 1(4)(b) probably does not provide sufficient reason to depart from the normal meaning.

2.6.3 Boundary wall

The normal meaning of this expression is a wall which marks a boundary, whether it stands on it or next to it, and whether it is the external wall of a building or free-standing. It is clear from the express qualifications attached to it in s 2(1) (where it means only a party fence wall or the external wall of a building) and s 1(1)(b) (where those meanings are excluded) that the Act uses it in this broad, general sense. This is the sense it must bear when it is used without qualification (eg s 2(2)(g)).

---

6 Section 7(2).
7 Section 8.

2.6.4 Line of junction

The Act fights shy of the word 'boundary', except in the expression 'boundary wall' and uses this periphrasis instead. No doubt, this is in order to emphasise that what is meant is an incorporeal concept rather than any physical feature.

2.7 EXTENT

In general, it is clear that walls and structures are only party walls, party fence walls, and party structures to the extent that they satisfy the statutory definitions. In the case of paragraph (b) party walls, this appears expressly from the words 'so much of'. Thus, a wall which is a party wall not because it stands astride the boundary, but only because the neighbour's building is built against it, is a party wall only where it adjoins the neighbour's building: those parts of the wall which project above, or to either side of, the neighbour's building are not a party wall.[8] The same must apply to a party structure, so that the horizontal structure dividing two flats, the lower of which projects further sideways than the higher, will not be a party structure to the extent that it projects and forms the roof of the lower flat.

2.8 MULTIPLE OWNERS

The building owner, who wishes to exercise his statutory rights, may or may not own part of the party wall (in a paragraph (b) case, it may belong entirely to the adjoining owner). In a simple case, the building owner will have only one adjoining owner to deal with, owning all the adjoining land. But if the party wall is the flank wall of a block of flats, there may be many persons who qualify as adjoining owners, including the landlord, the tenants of adjoining flats, and purchasers from either. The building owner will have to serve the requisite notices on all of them,[9] and they will all be entitled to participate in the procedure leading to an award.

---

8 See *Weston v Arnold* (1873) LR 7 Ch App 1084, *Drury v Army and Navy Auxiliary Co-operative Supply Ltd* [1896] 2 QB 271, *Knight v Pursell* (1879) 11 Ch D 412, *London Glos & N Hants Dairy Co v Morley & Lanceley* [1911] 2 KB 257. See also Figure 1.
9 See *Fillingham v Wood* [1891] 1 Ch 5; *Crosby v Alhambra Co Ltd* [1907] 1 Ch 295. For joint owners see para **13.8**.

Chapter 3

RIGHTS OF BUILDING OWNER

3.1 INTRODUCTION

The substantive provisions of the Act, giving rights to building owners, are ss 1 and 2. It should be emphasised that these rights are conditional on the operation of the statutory machinery. Until an initiating notice has been served, and, if a dispute ensues, until an award has been made under s 10, the building owner has only his rights at common law (see *Louis v Sadiq* (1996) *The Times*, 22 November, CA; *Upjohn v Seymour Estates Ltd* (1938) 54 TLR 465. The choice between ss 1 and 2 depends on whether the boundary between the adjoining owners has or has not been built upon already.

3.2 BOUNDARY NOT BUILT ON: SECTION 1

If the boundary is not built on at all (s 1(1)(a)), or is built on only to the extent of a boundary wall which is not a party fence wall nor the external wall of a building (s 1(1)(b)),[1] s 1 will apply. The building owner can use the section to acquire the right to build either: (a) a party wall or party fence wall on the boundary; or (b) a wall constructed wholly on his own land.

3.3 BUILDING ON THE BOUNDARY

If the building owner wishes to build a boundary wall astride the boundary (ie a party wall or a party fence wall), he must follow the procedure prescribed by s 1(2), (3) and (4).

3.3.1 Originating notice

First, the building owner must serve a notice under s 1(2). There are four requirements:

(a) it must be served at least one month before the building owner intends the building work to start;

(b) it must be served on 'any' adjoining owner, ie all those whose land adjoins the intended work;

---

1 It is difficult to see what this subsection adds beyond the case of a free-standing wall whose footings or foundations project beyond the boundary. The internal wall of attached houses is not within the words, since even if the wall is not built on the boundary, the house on the boundary side must be.

(c) it must indicate the building owner's desire to build;

(d) it must describe the intended wall.

Once the notice has been served under s 1(2), the building owner's rights depend on whether the adjoining owner serves on him a notice indicating his consent to the building of the proposed wall.

3.3.2   Consent notice

If the adjoining owner, having been duly served with notice under s 1(2), serves in response a notice indicating his consent to the building of the proposed wall, two consequences follow under s 1(3).

(a) The wall can be built. The two owners can agree its precise position, but unless they agree otherwise the building owner has a right to build it half on the land of each owner, ie centrally over the boundary.

(b) The second consequence is in respect of the cost of building the wall. Since the initiative comes from the building owner, it might be expected that he would normally have to pay all the costs. But the adjoining owner does not have to consent, and if he does it will presumably be because he considers the proposal advantageous to himself. A wall which is built partly on the adjoining owner's land will belong partly to him, and it will be of some use to the adjoining owner, even if only for supporting climbing plants. This is the philosophy behind s 1(3)(b), under which the costs are to be shared by the two owners in proportions which have regard to the use 'made or to be made' of the wall by each of them. Nor is this initial sharing a once-for-all arrangement. The costs are to be shared 'from time to time', so that if one owner later makes greater use of the wall than was originally contemplated, he becomes liable to pay a further contribution. All contributions are assessed according to the cost of labour and materials prevailing at the time of assessment. This is one of the contingent liabilities imposed by the Act, which are considered in more detail later.[2] What may be noted here is that it can fall on either party, and can occur an unlimited number of times.

These consequences may or may not be regarded as equitable. The adjoining owner needs to appreciate that they are the terms to which he is agreeing, if he serves a consent notice.

3.3.3   No consent

If the adjoining owner does not serve a notice of consent within 14 days of the service on him of the building owner's notice under s 1(2), s 1(4) will apply. The building owner can build the wall, but entirely at his own expense, and

----

2 See paras **14.10–14.14**.

wholly on his own land. For further consequences see paras **3.4.2** and **3.4.3**. The wall will no doubt be a 'work in pursuance of this Act' within s 8(1), so that the building owner will be entitled to exercise the statutory rights of entry for the purpose of executing the work.

3.3.4 Late consent

Some confusion seems to arise from the time-limit imposed on consent by s 1(4) (which is new). No such limit is imposed by s 1(3), so that a consent notice at any time appears to satisfy that section. But only a notice of consent within the 14-day period will satisfy s 1(4), and in default the building owner 'may only' proceed as authorised by that section. Could the building owner rely on a late consent notice, served after, say, 3 weeks? In view of the strictness with which the courts have approached the machinery of this legislation,[3] the prudent building owner may wish to start again with a fresh notice under s 1(2), giving the adjoining owner another opportunity to serve a consent notice satisfying s 1(4).

3.4 WALL WHOLLY ON BUILDING OWNER'S LAND

If the building owner wishes from the outset to build a boundary wall wholly on his own land, he must serve a notice on the adjoining owner under s 1(5), not 1(2). At first sight this is surprising. Sections 1(1) and (5) apply only if the building owner intends to build on the boundary ('the line of junction' in the words of the Act). Why must he serve a notice, if he intends to build wholly on his side of the boundary? The answer lies in the footings and foundations, as is demonstrated by s 1(6). It is clear that a wall will, for the purposes of s 1, be wholly on the building owner's land even if it has footings and foundations which project into the adjoining owner's land. But the footings and foundations of such a wall will be built on the boundary, and it will therefore fall within s 1(1) and (5). If the building owner intends to build not only the wall but its footings and foundations as well wholly on his land, s 1 will not apply, and no notice need be served under it, but the building owner will then presumably be effectively abandoning a strip of his land to the adjoining owner. He may need to serve a 3- or 6-metre notice under s 6.[4]

The distinction between building 'on the line of junction' (s 1(2)) and building 'on the line of junction a wall placed wholly on his own land' (s 1(5)) lacks precision, so that it is not always easy to tell which section applies. If the adjoining owner's existing wall is hard up against, but not on, the boundary, s 1 must apply. If the building owner wishes to build right up against the existing wall, that will be wholly on his own land, so that he can proceed under s 1(5).

---

3 See *Gyle-Thompson v Wall Street (Properties) Ltd* [1974] 1 All ER 295.
4 See Chapter 4.

But what if he wishes to key his new structure into the existing wall? It is considered that this is not permissible under s 1(5), since the new structure will to some extent project across the boundary (above the level of the footings). It follows that a notice under s 1(2) is needed, which is likely to lead to a dispute, since consenting will probably not be acceptable to the adjoining owner (in view of s 1(3)(a)), and building wholly on his own land (under s 1(4)(b)) will not be acceptable to the building owner.

3.4.1   Originating notice

The requirements for a notice under s 1(5) are exactly the same as those for a notice under s 1(2) (see para **3.3.1**). The section does not interfere with the building owner's right to build on his own land, and there is no provision for consent or non-consent by the adjoining owner (but see para **3.5**). But there are two prescribed consequences, which apply whether the wall is built wholly on the building owner's land under s 1(4) (see para **3.3.3**) or s 1(5).

3.4.2   Footings and foundations

The first consequence is that under s 1(6) the building owner has the right within a defined period to place underground in the adjoining owner's land such projecting footings and foundations as are necessary for the construction of the walls. The defined period begins one month after the service of the building owner's notice under s 1(2) or (5), as the case may be, and continues for one year.

3.4.3   Cost and compensation

The second consequence is financial (under s 1(7)). The building owner must build at his own expense, and must compensate any adjoining owner or occupier for any damage to his property occasioned by the building of the wall, and the placing of projecting footings or foundations in the adjoining owner's land under s 1(6).

3.5   DISPUTES

Any dispute arising from the procedures under s 1 is to be determined in accordance with s 10 (s 1(8)). But, in contrast to s 2 (see para **3.10**), there is no provision for deemed disputes to arise.

3.6   BOUNDARY ALREADY BUILT ON: SECTION 2

Where the boundary has already been built on (and this includes the case of all party walls), or there is at the line of the boundary a boundary wall which is a party fence wall or the external wall of a building,[5] s 2 will apply. The building owner can use s 2 to acquire rights to do works to the party (fence) wall or structure, which he would not have at common law. These rights are enumerated, and closely defined, in 13 subsections, and some of them are subjected to special conditions. In order to acquire these rights, the building owner must first serve a 'party structure notice' (s 3), to which the adjoining owner may respond with a counter-notice (under s 4).

3.7 RIGHTS UNDER SECTION 2

The rights which the building owner can acquire under s 2 are as follows (s 2(2)).

(a) The right to underpin, thicken or raise: (i) a party structure; (ii) a party fence wall; or (iii) an external wall which belonged to the building owner and is built against (i) or (ii).

If work pursuant to this right is necessitated by a defect or want of repair of the structure or wall concerned, no special conditions are attached to the exercise of the right. If not, however, the following conditions are imposed (by s 2(3)):[6]

(i) all damage occasioned by the work to the adjoining premises or to their internal furnishings and decorations must be made good;

(ii) there is special protection for flues and chimney stacks which belong to the adjoining owner and either form part of, or rest on or against, the structure or wall affected. They must be carried up to a height agreed by the adjoining owner, or determined under s 10, and the materials used for doing so must be similarly agreed or determined.

Section 11(4) makes special provision for expenses incurred in exercising this right (see para **11.4.2**).

(b) The right to make good, repair, or demolish and rebuild, a party structure or party fence wall, where such work is necessitated by a defect or want of repair of the structure or wall.

Section 11(5) makes special provision for expenses incurred in exercising this right (see para **11.4.3**).

(c) The right to demolish a partition which separates buildings belonging to different owners but does not conform with statutory requirements, and to build instead a party wall which does so conform.

---

5 This includes the case of an external wall of a building which stands wholly on one owner's land, but with footings projecting into the neighbour's land.

6 For further reference to the conditions imposed by s 2, see Chapter 6.

Throughout s 2, references to 'statutory requirements' import a special meaning. Buildings and structures which were erected before the passing of the Act (18 July 1996) are deemed to conform with statutory requirements if they conformed with the statutes regulating buildings or structures at the time when they were erected (s 2(8)). This right, therefore, is not applicable to such buildings and structures. But it will be applicable to buildings and structures erected after 18 July 1996, even though they conformed with statutory requirements when they were first built, if the statutory requirements are subsequently tightened.

(d) The right in the case of buildings connected by arches or structures over public ways, or over passages belonging to other persons, to demolish the whole or part of such buildings, arches or structures which do not conform with statutory requirements and to rebuild them so that they do so conform.

(e) The right to demolish a party structure which is of insufficient strength or height for the purposes of any intended building of the building owner, and to rebuild it of sufficient strength or height for those purposes (including rebuilding to a lesser height or thickness where the rebuilt structure is of sufficient strength and height for the purposes of any adjoining owner). This right is subject to the same conditions as affect right (a) above (s 2(4)). It is also subject to a special obligation to pay compensation for disturbance if the adjoining premises are laid open.[7] The express right to rebuild to a lesser height reverses the decision of law in *Gyle-Thompson v Wall Street (Properties) Ltd* [1974] 1 All ER 295, but in view of the proviso safeguarding the purposes of the adjoining owner, a decision on similar facts might well be the same (since the lowering of the party wall diminished the adjoining owner's privacy).

Section 11(6) makes special provision for the payment of compensation when premises are laid open in the exercise of this right (see para **6.7**).

(f) The right to cut into a party structure for any purpose (which may be, or include, the purpose of inserting a damp proof course). This right is subject to the condition that all damage occasioned by the work to the adjoining premises or to their internal furnishings and decorations must be made good (s 2(5)).

(g) The right to cut away from a party wall, party fence wall, external wall or boundary wall any footing or any projecting chimney breast, jamb or flue, or other projection on or over the land of the building owner in order to erect, raise or underpin any such wall or for any other purpose. This right is subject to the same condition as (f).

---

7 Section 11(6): see Chapter 6.

(h) The right to cut away or demolish parts of any wall or building of an adjoining owner overhanging the land of the building owner or overhanging a party wall, to the extent that it is necessary to cut away or demolish the parts to enable a vertical wall to be erected or raised against the wall or building of the adjoining owner. This right is subject to the same condition as (f).

(j) The right to cut into the wall of an adjoining owner's building in order to insert a flashing or other weather-proofing of a wall erected against that wall. This right is subject to the condition that all damage occasioned by the work to the wall of the adjoining owner's building must be made good (s 2(6)).

(k) The right to execute any other necessary works incidental to the connection of a party structure with the premises adjoining it.

(l) The right to raise a party fence wall, or to raise such a wall for use as a party wall, and to demolish a party fence wall and rebuild it as a party fence wall or as a party wall.

(m) The right to reduce, or to demolish and rebuild, a party wall or party fence wall to: (i) a height of not less than 2 metres where the wall is not used by an adjoining owner to any greater extent than a boundary wall; or (ii) a height currently enclosed upon by the building of an adjoining owner. This right is subject to the condition that: (i) if there is an existing parapet, it must be reconstructed or replaced; or (ii) if not, a parapet must be constructed where one is needed (s 2(7)). If the adjoining owner by counter-notice requires the existing height of the wall to be maintained, he must pay a due proportion of the cost, so far as it exceeds the specified heights (s 11(7)).

(n) The right to expose a party wall or party structure hitherto enclosed, subject to providing adequate weathering.

3.8 PARTY STRUCTURE NOTICE

If the building owner can obtain the written consent of all adjoining owners and adjoining occupiers, he can exercise any of the rights conferred by s 2 without further formality (s 3(3)(a)). If he is served with a notice under the legislation relating to dangerous or neglected structures,[8] he can proceed without serving a party structure notice (s 3(3)(b)), if he has power to do the work under that legislation or otherwise.[9] Subject to those exceptions, however, he cannot exercise any of the rights granted by s 2 without first serving on any adjoining owner a party structure notice under s 3.

---

8 For example, the Building Act 1984, ss 76–83.

9 This dispensation applies only to work required by the statutory notice served on the building owner: see *Spiers and Son Ltd v Troup* (1915) 84 LJKB 1986.

3.8.1 Requirements

The requirements of a party structure notice are as follows (s 3(1)):

(a) it must state the name and address of the building owner;

(b) it must state the nature and particulars of the proposed work. If the building owner is proposing to construct special foundations,[10] it must include plans, sections and details of construction of the special foundations, together with reasonable particulars of the loads to be carried by them;

(c) it must state the date on which the proposed work will begin;

(d) it must be served at least two months before the date on which the proposed work is to begin (s 3(2)(a)).

3.8.2 Effect

A party structure notice is the first step towards enabling the building owner to exercise a right under s 2. The next step will depend on the response of the adjoining owner, who may react in one of three ways.

(a) If within 14 days of the service on him of the party structure notice the adjoining owner serves on the building owner a notice indicating his consent (under s 5), there is no dispute and the building owner can proceed without further formality to carry out the works described in the party structure notice.

(b) The adjoining owner may within one month of service of the party structure notice serve on the building owner a counter-notice, in which case s 4 will apply.

(c) The adjoining owner may take neither of these steps, in which case there is a deemed dispute (under s 5), which has to be resolved under s 10.

In any event, a party structure notice ceases to have effect if the work to which it relates: (i) is not begun within the calendar year beginning on the date of its service;[11] and (ii) is not prosecuted with due diligence (s 3(2)(b)). If it ceases to have effect, the building owner must start again by serving a new party structure notice.[12]

---

10 Ie foundations in which an assemblage of beams or rods is employed for the purpose of distributing any load: s 20. See further Chapter 5.

11 But this time-limit does not apply where there is a reference to surveyors within the year: see *Leadbetter v Marylebone Corp* [1905] 1 KB 661 and para **4.8**.

12 For a discussion of the 'due diligence' requirement, see para **4.9**.

3.9   COUNTER-NOTICE: SECTION 4

An adjoining owner who has been duly served with a party structure notice may serve a counter-notice on the building owner under s 4.

3.9.1   Objects

There are two legitimate objects of a counter-notice, which appear from the matters which have to be set out in it (s 4(1)).

(a) The adjoining owner can require modifications for his own reasonable convenience in the building owner's proposals in respect of a party fence wall or party structure. He may require the building owner to build in or on the wall or structure such chimney copings, breasts, jambs, or flues, or such piers or recesses or other like works, as may reasonably be required for his convenience. For example, when the building owner is proposing to reduce the height of a wall, the adjoining owner can require him to maintain its existing height (s 11(7)).

(b) The second object concerns special foundations.[13] The building owner will have no right to install special foundations without the adjoining owner's consent in writing (s 7(4)). If he is prepared to consent subject to modifications, he can in the counter-notice require that they: (i) be placed at a specified greater depth than that proposed by the building owner; or (ii) be constructed of sufficient strength to bear the load to be carried by columns of any building which he may intend to build.

3.9.2   Requirements

There are two requirements for a counter-notice (s 4(2)).

(a) It must specify the works (in the categories mentioned in para **3.9.1**) which the adjoining owner requires to be executed, and must be accompanied by plans, sections and particulars of such works.

(b) It must be served within the month beginning on the date of service of the party structure notice.

3.9.3   Effect

Prima facie the building owner is bound to comply with the requirements set out in a duly served counter-notice, but he is not bound to comply if the works required would: (a) be injurious to him; (b) cause unnecessary inconvenience to him; or (c) cause unnecessary delay in the execution of the works pursuant to the party structure notice (s 3(3)). There are two courses open to the building owner.

---

13 See Chapter 5.

(a) If he is content with the requirements set out in the counter-notice, he can within 14 days serve a notice indicating his consent (under s 5), in which case he can proceed with the works in the party structure notice, as modified by the counter-notice, without further formality.

(b) He can abstain from serving a notice of consent, in which case there is a deemed dispute, which must be resolved under s 10 (s 5).

The adjoining owner has to pay the expenses of carrying out works required by his counter-notice (see s 11(9) and para **11.4.5**).

3.10   DISPUTES: SECTION 5

An owner who is served with a party structure notice or a counter-notice can serve a notice indicating his consent within 14 days. In default of any such consent notice, a dispute is deemed to arise under s 5, which must be resolved under s 10.

Chapter 4

ADJACENT EXCAVATION AND CONSTRUCTION

4.1 INTRODUCTION

Unlike ss 1 and 2, which enlarge the building owner's rights, the principal effect of s 6 of the Act is to restrict his right to conduct operations wholly on his own land. It applies where a building owner proposes to carry out excavations or to excavate for and erect a building or structure within certain distances of any building belonging to an adjoining owner. All owners of buildings within the specified distances are adjoining owners (s 6(4)). The building owner must serve an initiating notice, and unless a notice of consent is served a dispute is deemed to have arisen between the building owner and the adjoining owner, which is referred for an award under s 10.

Section 6 contains two separate provisions, according to the distance within which the adjacent excavation is to be carried out from the building of the adjoining owner. Section 6(1) deals with excavation within 3 metres of the building, and s 6(2) applies where the work is to be carried out within 6 metres of the building. These provisions reproduce (in metric form) the provisions of s 50 of the 1939 Act, where the relevant distances were 10 feet and 20 feet respectively.

4.2 3-METRE NOTICE

Section 6(1) of the Act is derived from s 50(1)(a) of the 1939 Act. It applies where any excavation building or structure is within 3 metres measured horizontally from any part of a building or structure of the adjoining owner if the excavation proposed will, within the 3-metre limit, extend to a lower level than the bottom of the foundations of the building or structure of the adjoining owner.

4.3 6-METRE NOTICE

This is governed by s 6(2), which again reproduces a provision of the 1939 Act, namely s 50(1)(b), with the substitution of 6 metres for the 20 feet of the earlier provision. The section applies in the case of excavation works within 6 metres of the adjoining owner's building, where any part of the proposed excavation building or structure will within the 6 metres meet a plane drawn downwards in the direction of the excavation building or structure of the building owner at an angle of 45° to the horizontal from the line formed by the intersection of the plane of the level of the bottom of the foundations of the building or structure

6-Metre Notice

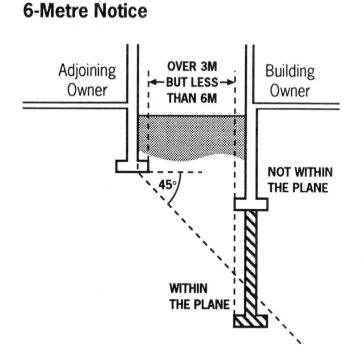

Figure 3

of the adjoining owner with the plane of the external face of the external wall of the building or structure of the adjoining owner.

These descriptions can be more easily understood from a diagram, see Figure 3 above. Note that the measurements are from the nearest points, which are assumed to be the projecting underground foundations.

4.4 EXCAVATION

'Excavation' involves hollowing out the ground, and does not include the demolition of a building which has a pre-existing cellar, even though the effect of such demolition is to leave the void created by the cellar exposed to the elements. On the other hand, if the retaining wall of the existing cellar is removed, to form the foundations and cellar walls of a new building, this will involve excavation. Presumably, the simple drilling of a small diameter hole into the ground, for example to take core samples, will not be excavation, but the construction of a large shaft will be. Further, it would seem excavation remains excavation even if it is backfilled or occupied by elements of the construction during the works.

4.5 BUILDING OR STRUCTURE

The reference to 'any part of a building or structure' applies, it is submitted, to foundations where, for example, the footings of the adjoining owner's building project beyond his flank wall, and to other underground parts such as deep piles. For this reason, it may often be difficult to ascertain whether the sections apply. Further, it is not clear whether an underground pipe or conduit falls within the definition of 'building or structure'. This may be of considerable practical importance, since the ownership of such drains and conduits may be difficult to determine, and their location may be virtually impossible to ascertain in advance. It is submitted that underground drains, conduits, and pipes are not within the definition, for the following reasons.

(a) The practical difficulties already mentioned. The section should not be construed so as to interfere unreasonably with the building owner's right to build on his own land.

(b) By contrast, ascertaining the relative position of the adjoining owner's building and the proposed excavation, and the distances between them, is straightforward.

(c) The stated intention of the Act was to introduce the 1939 Act regime to the whole country. Consideration of the 1939 Act as a whole suggests that such drains, pipes and conduits would not fall within the definition of a building or structure. For example, the provisions of Part VII of the 1939 Act relating to dangerous and neglected structures are not drafted in terms apt to apply to such items.[1]

4.6 SECTION 6(3)

Where excavation work is contemplated within the distance limits, the building owner is given the right to underpin or otherwise strengthen or safeguard the foundations of the building and structure of the adjoining owner so far as may be necessary (s 6(3)). He is also bound to do this, if required to by the adjoining owner. In either case, these operations must be at the expense of the building owner.[2] Note that the obligation is not limited to those parts of the adjoining owner's building which fall within the defined distances. The extent of work required must in the case of dispute be decided in accordance with s 10.

4.7 NOTICES

At least one month before beginning to excavate, the building owner must serve on the adjoining owner a notice indicating his proposals and stating

---

1 Although they are not specifically excluded; see the definition in s 60.

2 Notwithstanding s 11(9).

whether he proposes to underpin or otherwise strengthen or safeguard the foundations of the building or structure of the adjoining owner (s 6(5)). The notice must be accompanied by plans and sections showing the site and depth of any excavation the building owner proposes to make, and, if he proposes to erect a building or structure, its site (s 6(6)). If a consent by the adjoining owner is not served within 14 days, a dispute is deemed to have arisen (s 6(7)).

4.8 LAPSE OF NOTICE

A notice ceases to have effect if the work to which it relates has not begun within the period of 12 months beginning with the day on which the notice was served and is not prosecuted with due diligence (s 6(8)). The 12-month time-limit does not apply, if it expires while a dispute is still being resolved pursuant to s 10 (see *Leadbetter v Marylebone Corp* [1905] 1 KB 661).[3]

4.9 DUE DILIGENCE

It is considered that 'due diligence' involves the application of men, materials and plant industriously and efficiently towards the completion of the works.[4]

(a) If the work is not prosecuted with due diligence the notice by the building owner ceases to have effect. The notice is not rendered invalid *ab initio*, so that work already carried out under it does not cease to be authorised by the Act. But it appears that the right to carry out further work stops. No machinery is provided for reviving the right to proceed under the notice. It seems that the building owner can only serve a fresh notice.

(b) No provision is made about work already carried out. In practical terms, this raises a considerable difficulty if the work has been left in an unsafe or unsatisfactory state from the adjoining owner's point of view. The adjoining owner is given no right to sue for the expense of reinstatement, or for damages for failure to prosecute with due diligence. He would have to sue for damages under s 7(2) and (5) of the Act claiming the cost of reinstatement.

4.10 PLANS

On completion of any work under s 6, the building owner must, on request, supply the adjoining owner with particulars including plans and sections of the work (s 6(9)). The purpose of this is presumably to enable the adjoining owner

---

3 Although the wording of s 6(8)(a) is different from s 90(4) of the 1894 Act, it is not thought that the differences will affect this commonsense decision, which has stood for so long.

4 See *West Faulkner Associates v London Borough of Newham* (1995) 11 Const LJ 157, CA.

to plan any future work of his own, or to take appropriate remedial steps if structural distress subsequently occurs in his building. This provision creates a statutory duty, which would be enforceable by damages and (where appropriate) a mandatory injunction.

Chapter 5

SPECIAL FOUNDATIONS

5.1 INTRODUCTION

Special foundations are a side issue in the Act. They are not dealt with comprehensively, but they crop up in three separate contexts, which can conveniently be brought together.

5.2 DEFINITION

In s 20, special foundations are defined as:

> 'foundations in which an assemblage of beams or rods is employed for the purpose of distributing any load.'

In deference to modern methods of construction, the word 'steel' before 'beams' has been dropped. As it stands, the definition (which derives from s 44 of the 1939 Act) refers primarily to reinforced concrete and grillage foundations.

5.3 GENERAL PRINCIPLE

The general principle is that the Act does not authorise the building owner to place special foundations in the adjoining owner's land without his previous consent in writing (s 7(4)). The building owner may propose them, but the adjoining owner has an absolute right to veto them.

5.4 SECTIONS 1 AND 2

In accordance with the general principle, ss 1 and 2, although they contemplate projecting footings and foundations (s 1(6)) and underpinning (s 2(2)(a), (g)), do not give any right to construct special foundations in the adjoining owner's land.

5.5 PARTY STRUCTURE NOTICE

Nevertheless, it is one of the requirements of a party structure notice that, if the building owner proposes to construct special foundations, the notice must give full particulars of their construction and the loads they are to be designed to carry (s 3(1)(b)). Consistently with the general principle, it might be expected that such a proposal would be limited to special foundations to be constructed in the building owner's land. The next section, however, shows otherwise.

5.6 COUNTER-NOTICE

Section 4(1)(b) enables the adjoining owner to use his counter-notice for the purpose of consenting to a proposal for special foundations under s 7(4) while imposing requirements for his own advantage. The reference to s 7(4) shows that special foundations in the adjoining owner's land are meant here, because that section does not apply to special foundations in the building owner's land. Thus, the Act contemplates that the special foundations proposed in a party structure notice may legitimately include special foundations in the adjoining owner's land. The requirements which the adjoining owner can impose in his counter-notice under s 4(1)(b) are:

(a) that the foundations be placed at a specified greater depth than that proposed by the building owner; and

(b) that they be constructed of sufficient strength to bear the load to be carried by columns of any building which the adjoining owner may intend to build on his land.

Thus, the adjoining owner can impose conditions requiring the special foundations to be strong enough for his own future purposes. The building owner must comply unless one of the exceptions in s 3(3) is applicable.[1]

5.7 EXPENSES

In general, the building owner must bear the expenses of special foundations which he proposes. But there are two special provisions in s 11.

5.7.1   Section 11(9)

Under s 11(9)(b), the adjoining owner is liable for the expenses of carrying out works 'requested or required' by him. Expenses he has 'required' will include additional expenses caused by any requirement which he has imposed in respect of special foundations under s 4(1)(b), but not the expense of underpinning which he has required (see s 6(3)).

5.7.2   Section 11(10)

Section 11(10) deals specifically with special foundations. It applies where an adjoining owner has consented to the construction of special foundations on

---

1 See para **3.9.3**.

his land, and when he later constructs a building on his land its cost is increased by their existence. In such a case, the adjoining owner can, after completion of the work, claim so much of the cost as was due to the existence of the special foundations from the owner of the building to which they belong. In order to make this claim he must (as under s 13), within 2 months of the completion of the work, ensure that the responsible owner receives an account together with any necessary invoices and other supporting documents. This provision gives rise to a number of difficulties.

This is one of the contingent liabilities imposed by the Act. Like the others,[2] it gives rise to questions relating to benefit and burden.

(a) Burden

The burden is carefully imposed not on the building owner, but on 'the owner of the building to which the foundations belong'. This shows that the burden falls on the owner at the material time, and is not personal to the original building owner who installed the special foundations. Thus, like the other contingent liabilities, it may fall on a purchaser without notice who had no reliable means of discovering it.

(b) Benefit

The benefit is even more problematical. If the burden falls on future owners, one would expect the benefit to run with the adjoining owner's land. The language, however, is ill-suited to this result. The person entitled is 'the adjoining owner', and this must mean the adjoining owner who fulfils the condition in s 11(10)(b) by erecting the building on his land. Clearly, the original adjoining owner who fulfilled the condition in s 11(10)(a), by consenting to the foundations, will qualify. But what if it is a successor who does the building? Can he be 'the adjoining owner' within s 11(10)(b)? It is hard to wrest this meaning from the words. 'Adjoining owner' is defined (s 20) by reference to his relation to the building owner, who is in turn defined by his desire to exercise rights under the Act. Thus, in the context of s 11(10)(b), there is no current building owner or adjoining owner: 'the adjoining owner' can only be a description of the original adjoining owner by his former status. If his successor had been intended to be included, the expression should have been 'the owner of that land' (ie the land mentioned in s 11(10)(a)). This, however, is the sense in which the words must be construed if they are to produce a rational result.[3]

There are other ways in which the wording of this section is unsatisfactory.

(a) The concept of foundations 'belonging' to a building is imprecise. The Act itself contemplates that the adjoining owner may make use of special foundations constructed in his land by the building owner.[4] If he does so,

---

2 See Chapter 14, para **14.10**.
3 See further, para **14.2**.
4 See s 4(1)(b)(ii).

but later finds that those foundations hinder building operations on his land (eg demolition and redevelopment), it is unclear whether they 'belong' to the neighbouring building sufficiently to support total, or even partial, liability for the increased expenses.

(b) It is not provided that the account must be served on the owner responsible (ie under s 15), but liability arises only if he *receives* it within the time-limit. Service and receipt are not the same thing. Part of the object of machinery for service is to enable service to be proved whether a document has actually been received or not. It seems the expense and embarrassment of personal service may be needed.

(c) In contrast to s 13(2), no provision is made for objections to the account nor for determination under s 10. No doubt this will be a matter within the jurisdiction of the surveyors, if any notice has been served under the Act. But the operations are, *ex hypothesi*, on the adjoining owner's land, and he may not have needed to serve any notice. In that case, it is not clear whether there is jurisdiction under s 10 (the deeming in s 13(2) suggests otherwise), or only in the court.

Chapter 6

ANCILLARY RIGHTS AND OBLIGATIONS

6.1 INTRODUCTION

Section 7 of the Act imposes duties on the building owner, regulating the exercise of his rights under the Act, and gives valuable rights to the adjoining owner. This chapter also deals with the building owner's obligations to make good any damage (under s 2) and to pay compensation.

6.2 SECTION 7

Section 7 groups together five subsections, whose unifying thread is that they are designed to protect adjoining owners. But they do not develop logically, and some are general, some specific.

(a) Subsections (1) and (2) are general, and protect adjoining occupiers as well as owners. But subsection (1) (unnecessary inconvenience) is concerned with the way rights are exercised (ie the carrying out of works), while (2) (compensation) is also concerned with the effect of works once executed.

(b) Subsection (3) (hoardings etc) gives specific protection, again to occupiers as well as owners, while work is proceeding, when it has the effect of 'laying open' the adjoining land or building.

(c) Subsection (4) is concerned with special foundations, and is dealt with in Chapter 5.

(d) Subsection (5) (plans) controls the works which can be carried out, as between building owner and adjoining owner.

It is convenient to start with the subsections which are concerned with the carrying out of work, namely (5), (1) and (3).

6.3 SECTION 7(5): WHAT WORK MAY BE CARRIED OUT

This subsection is an essential part of the machinery of the Act, operating between building owner and adjoining owner. It strictly defines what work the building owner can carry out.

(a) The works must comply with statutory requirements. The obvious requirements are those of the Building Regulations, and the Building Act 1984. But all other relevant statutory provisions, are included. For example, the provisions of the Control of Pollution Act 1974 regarding noise on construction sites, and of the Health and Safety at Work etc Act 1974 and Regulations regarding site safety (eg the Construction (Design and Management) Regulations 1994).

(b) There must be plans, sections and particulars, which may be agreed between the owners or determined by an award (under s 10), and the works must be executed in accordance with them.

(c) There can be no deviation from the plans, except such as may be agreed between the owners (or between surveyors acting on their behalf), or determined by a further award.

6.4   SECTION 7(1): UNNECESSARY INCONVENIENCE

This subsection provides that a building owner shall not exercise any right conferred on him by the Act in such manner or at such time as to cause unnecessary inconvenience to any adjoining owner or occupier.

This is a general obligation restricting the way the defined works are to be carried out. It may be expressly embodied in the award, but it will apply even if it is not.

The inclusion of adjoining occupiers extends the benefit to tenants and other residents who do not satisfy the definition of owners.[1] They will not have had any right to participate in the determination under s 10, but their interests are to some extent protected by s 7.

The concept of unnecessary inconvenience appears to impose a stricter duty than the tort of nuisance, where the criterion is unreasonable interference with the enjoyment of land. An interference may be reasonable, but not necessary, and a method of working may cause inconvenience without amounting to an interference.[2] No doubt there must, as in the law of nuisance, be a balancing of the interests of the parties.[3] There is a breach of this duty if the building owner delays unreasonably in rebuilding a party wall.[4]

6.5   SECTION 7(3): BUILDING LAID OPEN

This subsection imposes a specific obligation on the building owner, when his operations under the Act involve laying open any part of the adjoining land or building. He must provide, for as long as may be necessary, a proper hoarding, shoring, fans or temporary structure for the protection of the land or building, and the security of any adjoining occupier.

---

1 See para **2.5**.
2 See *Clerk and Lindsell on Torts* (17th edn) para 18.12, *Andreae v Selfridge & Co Ltd* [1938] Ch 1.
3 See eg *Leakey v National Trust* [1980] QB 485.
4 See *Jolliffe v Woodhouse* (1894) 10 TLR 553.

This provision is necessitated by the very radical works which may be authorised under the Act, involving, it may be, the removal of a wall which exposes the interior of the adjoining building. In such a case the award will no doubt make provision for protection of the adjoining occupiers, but that will not detract from this duty: if the measures provided by the award are not adequate, the building owner must still do what is necessary for protection and security; and should be alive to this obligation.

The need where a building is exposed is obvious. But it is less obvious where it is just part of the land which is 'laid open'. Even a modest trench for the purposes of installing footings involves, in ordinary language, a laying open of the land. It is considered that the use of the word 'proper' indicates that there is no need to provide hoardings etc unless they are appropriate. A deep trench may need support to prevent subsidence; a shallow one may not require any special measures.

Laying open premises also gives rise to liability for disturbance and inconvenience under s 11(6).[5]

6.6   SECTION 7(2): COMPENSATION

This subsection, which is new, imposes an obligation on the building owner to compensate adjoining owners and occupiers for any loss or damage which may result to them 'by reason of any work executed in pursuance of the Act'.[6]

It seems clear that the loss or damage covered by this provision includes that caused by the existence of the work, once executed, for example any diminution in the value of the adjoining owner's property.

It is not altogether clear whether damage suffered during the course of the work (eg physical damage to the adjoining premises) is also covered. There is an ambiguity in the words quoted above. The 'work' may be limited to the finished object produced by working,[7] or it may embrace the doing of the work. It is submitted that the context is capable of supporting the second, wider, meaning, and that the wider construction is to be preferred. An important factor pointing in this direction is the position of the adjoining occupier. Whereas the adjoining owner may be protected by specific provisions in the award, the occupier has only the statute to protect him.

It is therefore considered that compensation can be awarded under the section both for the temporary effects of carrying out the work and for the permanent effects of the finished work. In general, this appears to cover at least as much ground as damages for nuisance.

---

5 See para **6.7**.

6 A welcome innovation, overruling *Adams v Marylebone BC* [1907] 2 KB 822, which decided that works authorised by the 1894 Act could not give rise to compensation.

7 The word is used in this sense in eg s 14(2).

6.7   SECTION 11(6): ALLOWANCE FOR DISTURBANCE

In addition, s 11(6) provides that a building owner who lays open adjoining premises pursuant to s 2(2)(e) (ie by demolishing a party structure) must pay 'a fair allowance in respect of disturbance and inconvenience' to the adjoining owner and occupier.

The use of the expression 'fair allowance', rather than 'compensation', is strange. It goes back to the 1894 Act[8] (where it is not restricted to laying open), and may reflect an appreciation of the difficulty of translating disturbance and inconvenience into money. It is not thought that the expression means anything other than compensation here.

It is not clear how far this subsection adds to s 7(2), except by making it clear that disturbance and inconvenience are subjects for compensation.

6.8   CIVIL ENFORCEMENT

All the sections mentioned above (apart from s 7(5)) impose obligations for the benefit of adjoining owners and occupiers. If the building owner fails to perform these obligations it is considered that the adjoining owners and occupiers can enforce them by civil action for breach of statutory duty. Adjoining occupiers have no other means of enforcement. Adjoining owners may be protected also by overlapping obligations imposed in an award which can be separately enforced, but insofar as the award does not protect them to the same extent as the Act, it is considered that they are entitled to enforce the statutory obligations.[9]

6.9   DUTY TO MAKE GOOD

It has already been noticed that certain rights under s 2 are conditional.[10] The conditions imposed on the building owner consist of obligations: (a) to make good any damage; and (b) to carry out specified works. The rights and their respective conditions can be summarised in tabular form.

Right	*Conditions*
Section 2(2)(a): underpinning etc	Section 2(3). Unless work is necessitated by defect or want of repair: (a) make good; (b) specified works, if work to party structure or external wall.

---

8 Section 95(2)(b).
9 See further paras **9.6–9.9**.
10 See paras **3.6** and **3.7**.

Section 2(2)(e): demolition etc	Section 2(4): (a) make good; (b) specified works. (NB Also liability under s 11(6)).
Section 2(2)(f): cutting into (g): away from, etc (h): overhangs	Section 2(5). Make good.
Section 2(2)(j): Weather-proofing	Section 2(6). Make good.
Section 2(2)(m): Reducing height	Section 2(7). Specified works. (NB Liability for adjoining owner under s 11(7)).

6.10   SECTION 11(8): PAYMENT IN LIEU

Where the building owner has to make good specified damage by reason of the conditions mentioned above, the adjoining owner can require that the expenses of making good be determined under s 10 and paid to him in lieu of carrying out the work (s 11(8)).

(a) The adjoining owner has an absolute right to make the requirement. The surveyors have no jurisdiction to enquire into its reasonableness.

(b) The section does not say that the requirement must be in writing, but it clearly should be. It does not have to be served in any particular way.

(c) The requirement cannot be made until it has been determined that works are to be carried out which are conditional on making good. It must clearly be made promptly after that, and certainly before the building owner embarks on making good.

(d) The right applies where the building owner has to 'make damage good', and applies only to the expenses of 'making good'. It does not appear to apply to the further expenses of the specified works mentioned above, even if the adjoining owner does not wish them to be carried out.

Chapter 7

RIGHTS OF ENTRY

7.1 INTRODUCTION

Section 8 confers rights of entry on land in favour of the building owner and the surveyors, subject to the prior service of notice. These rights are exercisable against occupiers as well as adjoining owners.

7.2 RIGHT OF BUILDING OWNER

Section 8(1) entitles the building owner to enter any land or premises for the purpose of executing work pursuant to the Act, and to remove any furniture or fittings or take any other action necessary for that purpose. The right may be exercised during usual working hours.

(a) The section expressly authorises the building owner to bring servants, agents, employees and workmen (who will include contractors and sub-contractors and their employees) onto the land. But they must be there for the purpose of executing work pursuant to the Act.

(b) The right is limited to executing work in pursuance of the Act. Therefore, there is no right to enter in respect of unrelated work even if it is part of the same project. Normally, the right will not be exercisable until the works pursuant to the Act have been defined by an award.

(c) The words at the end of the subsection 'take any other action necessary for that purpose' relate back to 'for the purpose of executing any work in pursuance of this Act' and not to the removal of any furniture or fittings. The only 'purpose' expressly referred to earlier in the subsection is the purpose of executing any work in pursuance of the Act.

7.3 RIGHT OF SURVEYORS

Under s 8(5), a surveyor is entitled to enter any land or premises during usual working hours for the purpose of carrying out the object for which he is appointed or selected.

(a) The purposes for which a surveyor is appointed or selected are the purposes of s 10, ie determination of a dispute. There is no right of entry for exploratory purposes, for example to determine whether a notice is necessary under s 6.

(b) In contrast to s 8(1), there is no express right for anyone other than the surveyor to enter. It is thought, however, that it may be legitimate for him to take an assistant for ministerial duties, such as measuring and note-taking.

7.4 NOTICE BEFORE ENTRY

It is an essential pre-condition to the exercise of these rights of entry that notice is served on all owners and occupiers of the land (s 8(3) or (6)). The methods of serving notices are dealt with in Chapter 13, and a precedent is provided in Appendix 4. At least 14 days' notice must be given, except in a case of emergency, when 'such notice of the intention to enter as may be reasonably practicable' is all that is required (s 8(3)(a), (6)(a)).

(a) 'Emergency' has been held to mean the sudden occurrence of facts causing an apprehension of danger or difficulty.[1] Examples might include unexpected movement in the party wall, collapse of excavations, etc.

(b) Subsections (3) and (6) are concerned with the length of notice required, and not its form. But it is considered that they cannot be satisfied by oral notice, since their references to 'serving' imply a document to be served under s 15. It follows that, even in an extreme emergency, a written notice must be handed over at the time of entry.

(c) 'Reasonably practicable' is not the equivalent of reasonable, nor does it mean simply what is reasonably capable physically of being done. It has been held to mean 'feasible in all the circumstances'.[2]

7.5 USUAL WORKING HOURS

Both rights are exercisable during 'usual working hours', which are not specified by the Act and give rise to some uncertainties. Whatever the meaning of this expression when the 1939 Act was passed, there has in recent years been a major change in the hours during which business activities are carried on. Retail stores are frequently open until late in the evening and, at least in major centres, trade 7 days a week. What limits are implied by the use of the expression today? The following suggestions are made.

(a) Since the hours must be 'usual', the hours worked by supermarkets or late night grocers etc, are irrelevant.

---

1 See *The Larchbank* [1943] AC 299.
2 Compare *Palmer v Southend-on-Sea Borough Council* [1984] 1 All ER 945, CA.

(b) The primary purpose of the limitation on hours is to protect adjoining owners and occupiers against unreasonable disturbance of their rest and privacy. The concept is of the hours between which a reasonable householder would regard it as usual for someone to be at work. Typically, it is thought, this would be under modern conditions between approximately 8.30 am and 5.30 pm 5 days per week. Saturday mornings might also be included, but not Sundays.[3]

(c) The concept may vary with the neighbourhood. What is usual in an industrial estate may differ from what is usual in a residential road.

7.6 CIVIL REMEDY

These rights of entry are enforceable by criminal sanctions under s 16.[4] Can they also be enforced by civil proceedings (ie declaration or injunction)?

(a) It is considered that s 8(1) is apt to create a private right in favour of the building owner, breach of which entitles him to seek relief from the civil courts.[5]

(b) On the other hand, it is considered that under s 8(5) the surveyors have no right. It is the building owner who has to serve the notice under s 8(6), so it appears to be his right which a surveyor exercises. Here too, therefore, it is the building owner who has a right of action if a surveyor is obstructed or denied entry.

7.7 OCCUPIERS

The adjoining owner whose land is entered will at least have had the opportunity to participate in the procedure leading to the award, and to make representations to the surveyors. Mere occupiers of the adjoining land are not so privileged. It may be that a 14-day notice, carrying a warning of potential criminal liability for obstruction, will be the first and only intimation that they are about to be seriously disturbed. The consolation provided by the Act is principally the right to compensation under s 7(2), and less importantly the further rights under s 7(1) and (3). In addition, an occupier who is a tenant with a qualified covenant for quiet enjoyment in the traditional form may, in some circumstances, have a claim against his landlord (the adjoining owner) for any interference with his possession. If the adjoining owner has opposed the

---

3 Under the Control of Pollution Act 1974, notices relating to noise caused by work on construction sites generally specify hours within these periods: see Control of Noise (Codes of Practice for Construction and Open Sites) Order 1984, SI 1984/1992.
4 See Chapter 16.
5 Compare *Solomons v R Gertzenstein Ltd* [1954] 2 All ER 625, CA.

award, or taken no part in the procedure, the building owner's entry will be by title paramount, and there will be no claim.[6] But if the adjoining owner has actively consented or agreed to operations which could not otherwise have been authorised, he may be liable for the interference.[7]

---

6 See *Kelly v Rogers* [1892] 1 QB 910.
7 Compare *Cohen v Tannar* [1900] 2 QB 609.

Chapter 8

THE AWARD – PROCEDURE AND SCOPE

8.1 INTRODUCTION

One of the principal features of the Act is the establishment of a special disputes resolution procedure. This is contained in s 10, derived from s 55 of the 1939 Act. When a dispute arises or is deemed to have arisen between building owner and adjoining owner, they must agree either jointly on the appointment of a single surveyor (called in the Act the 'agreed surveyor') or each must appoint a surveyor, and the two surveyors so appointed ('the parties' surveyors') must forthwith select a third surveyor (called in the Act the 'third surveyor') who is to resolve any disagreement between the parties' surveyors. The parties' surveyors and the third surveyor are known as the 'three surveyors'. In this book the expression 'the surveyors' is used to refer to the surveyor or surveyors acting under s 10, whichever procedure has been used. In practice, most disputes involve the three-surveyor procedure, but the third surveyor is rarely called in.

The status of surveyors is considered below. Although appointed (except in the case of a third surveyor) by the parties, they must act independently at all times. They should not regard the party who appointed them as their client, but simply as their 'appointing party'. The better view is that they are not arbitrators[1] and thus are, for example, under no duty to act judicially, to give reasons for their decisions, or comply with the Arbitration Act 1996. The mechanism by which the surveyors produce their decision is an award (or if necessary more than one award), which once issued and unless challenged on appeal (see Chapter 10) is final and binding on the parties.

8.2 DISPUTE

Section 10 is headed 'Resolution of Disputes', and it is the occurrence of a dispute which necessitates the appointment of surveyors. A dispute is a difference between a building owner and an adjoining owner in respect of any matter connected with any work to which the Act relates (s 10(1)). Disputes fall into three categories.

(a) There are many contexts in which the Act expressly contemplates the possibility of disputes arising and provides that they are to be resolved under s 10 (ss 1(8), 2(3)(b), 2(4)(b), 7(5)(b), 11(2), 12(1), 12(2)). Indeed, there is one context where the s 10 procedure is invoked without any reference to a dispute (s 11(8)).

---

1 See para **8.17**.

(b) The Act deems a dispute to arise in certain circumstances. Mostly, this occurs when a notice under the Act is not consented to (ss 5, 6(7)), but it also applies, perhaps unnecessarily, where the adjoining owner serves a notice of objection to an account from the building owner (s 13(2)).

(c) Actual disputes may arise which fall into neither of the foregoing categories.[2]

8.3   QUALIFICATION OF SURVEYORS

The Act does not require surveyors to be qualified in any particular way, or indeed at all. 'Surveyor' is defined simply as any person 'not being a party to the matter' appointed or selected under s 10 to determine disputes (s 20).

8.4   MACHINERY OF APPOINTMENT

There is elaborate machinery for the appointment and selection of surveyors. The following preliminary points may be noted.

(a) The Act uses the word 'appoint' for surveyors appointed by the parties, and 'select' for the selection of the third surveyor.[3]

(b) All appointments and selections must be in writing (s 10(2)).

(c) All appointments and selections 'shall not be rescinded by either party' (s 10(2)). This clearly makes appointments, which are made by the parties, irrevocable. Its effect on selections, however, is less clear, since they are not made by the parties, who would have no power to rescind them anyway.

8.5   METHODS OF APPOINTMENT AND SELECTION

The primary methods of appointment and selection are prescribed by s 10(1).

8.5.1   Agreed surveyor

The parties can concur in the appointment of a single surveyor (s 10(1)(a)). This is unusual, and normally the next subsection is followed.

8.5.2   Parties' surveyors

If there is no agreed surveyor, each party must appoint a surveyor (s 10(1)(b)).

---

2 See *Selby v Whitbread & Co* [1917] 1 KB 736 at 744–745.

3 But not consistently: the choice of the term 'appointing officer' (s 10(8)) is anomalous, and the reference to 'appointments' in the definition of this term (s 20) is a solecism.

8.5.3   Third surveyor

The two surveyors appointed by the parties must forthwith select the third surveyor (s 10(1)(b)).

8.6   SECONDARY METHODS

There are fall-back methods of appointment and selection, if the directions prescribed by s 10(1) are not followed.

8.6.1   Parties' surveyors

If either party to the dispute refuses to make an appointment under s 10(1)(b), or neglects to do so for 10 days after being served with a request by the other party, the other party may make the appointment on behalf of the defaulting party (s 10(4)). There appears to be nothing to prevent the other party appointing the surveyor he has already appointed himself, so as to convert him into an agreed surveyor. This procedure applies only to failure to appoint under s 10(1)(b), and apparently not to failure to appoint under s 10(5).[4]

8.6.2   Third surveyor

If either of the parties' surveyors refuses to select a third surveyor, or neglects to do so for 10 days after being served with a request by the other surveyor, the other surveyor can apply for the selection to be made by (a) the appointing officer[5] or, if the appointing officer or his employer is a party to the dispute, by (b) the Secretary of State (s 10(8)). This same procedure also applies if one of the parties' surveyors refuses or neglects to select a replacement third surveyor under s 10(9).[6]

8.7   DEATH AND INCAPACITY OF SURVEYORS

Once the surveyors have been duly appointed, the procedure under s 10 may nevertheless break down for a variety of reasons, which the section proceeds to cater for. The first group of reasons involve no question of fault. A surveyor may, before the dispute is settled: (a) die; (b) become incapable of acting (eg through supervening physical or mental incapacity);[7] or (c) deem himself incapable of acting. This last category is new, and seems to be designed to

---

4 See para **8.7.2**.
5 Ie the person appointed under the Act for the purpose by the local authority: s 20.
6 See para **8.8.2**.
7 For an illustration of incapacity in relation to arbitration see *Burkett Sharp & Co v East Cheap Dried Fruit Co* [1961] 2 Lloyd's Rep 80.

enable a surveyor to withdraw for any reason which he personally considers sufficient (eg ill health, overwork). The consequences vary according to the category of surveyor concerned.

8.7.1 Agreed surveyor

If it is an agreed surveyor who dies etc, the procedure under s 10 has to begin all over again (s 10(3)).

8.7.2 Parties' surveyors

If it is a surveyor appointed by a party, that party can appoint another surveyor in his place (s 10(5)). Steps taken by his predecessor are not invalidated, and he must presumably take up where the predecessor left off. If the party does not make the appointment, the other party does not appear to have power to make it on his behalf, since s 10(4) applies only to failure to appoint under s 10(1)(b).

8.7.3 Third surveyor

If it is the third surveyor, the other two surveyors must forthwith select another surveyor in his place (s 10(9)). If they fail to agree, either of them can invoke the secondary procedure under s 10(8).[8]

8.8 REFUSAL AND NEGLECT BY SURVEYORS

The procedure may also break down because a surveyor refuses or neglects to act. This too is provided for. In the cases of an agreed surveyor and a third surveyor, refusal and neglect are assimilated to death and incapacity.

8.8.1 Agreed surveyor

Thus if an agreed surveyor refuses to act, or neglects to do so for 10 days after being served with a request by either party, the procedure under s 10 has to begin all over again (s 10(3)).

8.8.2 Third surveyor

Similarly, if a third surveyor refuses to act, or neglects to do so for 10 days after being served with a request by either party or either party's surveyor, a new third surveyor must forthwith be selected (s 10(9)).

It should be noted that in these provisions there is a distinction between 'refuses to act' and 'neglects to act' after being served with a request. This

---

8 See para **8.6.2**.

repeated distinction throughout s 10 seems to imply that refusal involves an express refusal, whereas neglect merely involves inaction.

8.9   REFUSAL AND NEGLECT BY PARTIES' SURVEYORS

More elaborate provision is made in s 10(6) and (7) for refusal or neglect by the parties' surveyors. These sections apply to the parties' surveyors, whether appointed under s 10(1)(b), 10(4) or 10(5). They introduce the new and more rigorous concept of refusing or neglecting to act 'effectively'.

8.9.1   Section 10(6): refusal

Section 10(6) is very sweeping. If a surveyor refuses to act effectively, the other party's surveyor can proceed to act ex parte (ie on his own), and anything he does is as effectual as if he had been an agreed surveyor. In effect, therefore, the refusing surveyor is completely superseded by the other party's surveyor, who assumes the authority of an agreed surveyor, and is thus enabled to proceed to make an award on his own. There appears to be no opportunity for the refusing surveyor to retrieve his position: once the section applies he is completely ousted. It is considered that only very obstructive conduct could justify such a consequence. The contrast between refusing and neglecting suggests that there must be an express refusal to do something.[9] The word 'effectively' dilutes the refusal to some extent. It does not have to be a refusal to take any step at all (which may be what is necessary under s 10(3)(a) and 10(9)(a)), but a refusal to take any effective step. For example, it does not have to be 'I refuse to consider this matter at all', but might be 'I refuse to consider any plans embodying this proposal'. What is more difficult is the question whether a refusal to take a specific effective step (eg attending a meeting), as opposed to a refusal to take *any* effective step, could satisfy the section. On the whole, it is considered that a refusal related only to a specific step is more suitable to be dealt with under s 10(7).

8.9.2   Section 10(7): neglect

Under s 10(7), either party or one party's surveyor can serve on the other surveyor a request to take some action. If he does not act effectively within 10 days the requesting party's surveyor is entitled to act ex parte 'in respect of the subject matter of the request', and what he does will be as effectual as if he was an agreed surveyor. This is less draconian than s 10(6). It contemplates that the request will have a limited subject matter, and that the defaulting surveyor will be superseded only in respect of that subject matter. Again, the criterion is not total inaction but failure to take any effective step. This will include, for example, not only failure to answer correspondence at all, but also giving

---

9 See para **8.8.3**.

answers which amount to deliberate procrastination. It should be remembered, however, that if the request procedure is to be usefully exploited, the subject matter must be some concrete step which the requesting surveyor could effectually take on his own (eg appointing a third surveyor, or deciding a specific issue, such as security under s 12).

8.10   MAKING THE AWARD

The award is settled by:

(a)   the agreed surveyor, if there is one (s 10(1)); and if not

(b)   by the three surveyors (s 10(10)); or

(c)   by any two of them (s 10(10)). In practice, the award is normally settled jointly by the two surveyors appointed by the parties, who have recourse to the third surveyor only if they cannot reach agreement between themselves. Normally, therefore, the third surveyor takes an active part only if the other two do not agree, and his vote can then decide the issue.

But there is a fourth possibility:

(d)   either of the parties, or either of their surveyors can at any time call on the third surveyor to determine the disputed matters (s 10(11)). If this happens, the settling of the award is wholly in his hands.

8.11   SERVICE OF THE AWARD

Provision is made for the award, once it is made, to be served on the parties.

If the award is made by the parties' surveyors, they must serve it on the parties forthwith (s 10(14)).

If, however, the award is made by the third surveyor, he is under no obligation to serve it until after 'payment of the costs of the award': he must then serve it on either the parties or their surveyors, and if he chooses to serve on the surveyors, they in turn must forthwith serve it on the parties (s 10(15)). This is a new section, yet it is hard to accept that the phrase cited means what it says. In the context of s 10(13) (a), the natural meaning of 'the costs of the award' is the costs of making and obtaining the award, whose incidence will be determined by the award. These costs will be unquantified, and the paying party will not be known until the award is published. Yet s 10(15) requires them to be paid before the third surveyor parts with his award. This is absurd. The reference to 'the costs of the award' must be understood as a reference to the third surveyor's fees. The object is to assimilate his right to payment to that of an arbitrator.

8.12   SCOPE OF AWARD: SURVEYORS' JURISDICTION

Section 10 is concerned with disputes between a building owner and an adjoining owner 'in respect of any matter connected with any work to which this Act relates' (s 10(1)), and the subject matter of the award is, in general, described in exactly the same terms (s 10(10)). But s 10 is also more specific in prescribing the contents of an award.

The award may determine (s 10(12)):

(a)   the right to execute any work;

(b)   the time and manner of executing any work (but unless the parties agree, the time is not to start running until after the expiry of the minimum notice period prescribed by the Act);[10]

(c)   any other matter arising out of or incidental to the dispute, including the costs of making the award.

The award can also determine (s 10(13)) the incidence between the parties of the reasonable costs incurred in:

(a)   making or obtaining the award;

(b)   reasonable inspections of the work to which the award relates;

(c)   any other matter arising out of the dispute.

The words of s 10(12)(c) are deliberately wide. They are designed to give the surveyors jurisdiction not only over the subjects of dispute expressly mentioned in the Act,[11] but over any incidental question which can arise in the course of a dispute reuslting from the service of a notice under the Act. Thus they must determine not only the fundamental questions of what work is to be carried out, within what time, and with what precautions, but also ancillary questions such as what compensation is to be paid, what contributions made to expenses, and who is to pay the costs.

8.13   LIMITS OF JURISDICTION

There are, however, limits to the surveyors' jurisdiction in making their award. Their powers derive wholly from the Act, and if they travel outside those powers, the award may be wholly or partly void. A number of examples may be given.

(a)   The Act can be invoked only by the service of a valid initiating notice. If the initiating notice is invalid (eg because it is served in circumstances where the Act does not in truth apply), or has not been properly served on the

10   Ie 1 month for notices under ss 1 and 6, 2 months for notices under s 3.
11   See para **8.2**(a).

right party, any resulting award must be wholly void for want of jurisdiction.[12]

(b) Similarly, if a building owner carries out works and then serves a belated notice, but the premature works cause a disastrous collapse, the question of responsibility for the collapse arises purely at common law, and the surveyors have no jurisdiction to determine it by award under the Act.[13]

(c) An award cannot override the requirements of the Act, properly construed. Thus if an account is not served within the period allowed by s 13(2), no award can be based on it.[14]

(d) An award cannot authorise works which will permanently interfere with an easement of light, or otherwise infringe s 9.

(e) An award cannot direct a payment to be made to a person who is not entitled to it under the Act.[15]

(f) An award cannot authorise work under s 2 unless it falls within one of the descriptions in s 2(1).[16]

(g) An award cannot grant dispensation from the need to serve notice before carrying out work in the future.[17] It was thought to follow that an award could not impose continuing obligations, but the Court of Appeal has held that an award can impose an obligation to maintain a wall.[18]

8.14 SUCCESSIVE AWARDS

Section 10(10), which is new, has dropped the reference to settling matters in dispute 'from time to time during the continuance of the work'.[19] It was partly this phrase which enabled McCardie J to describe the jurisdiction of the surveyors as follows:

> 'Section 91 of the [1894] Act provides that the arbitrators ... shall settle *from time to time* all matters in dispute. Their jurisdiction is, I think, continuous and exclusive, subject to the rights of appeal. ... It remains unimpaired until the final adjustment of all questions in difference between the building owners who gave the notice and

---

12 See *Gyle-Thompson v Wall Street (Properties) Ltd* [1974] 1 All ER 295. The same applies if the surveyors are not properly appointed: ibid.

13 See *Woodhouse v Consolidated Property Corp* [1993] 1 EGLR 174, CA: it is not thought that the new wording of s 10(10) affects this decision. See also *Louis v Sadiq* (1996) *The Times*, 22 November, CA.

14 See *Spiers and Son Ltd v Troup* (1915) 849 LJKB 1986.

15 See *Re Stone and Hastie* [1903] 2 KB 463.

16 See *Gyle-Thompson v Wall Street (Properties) Ltd* [1974] 1 All ER 295.

17 See *Leadbetter v Marylebone Corp* [1904] 2 KB 893, CA.

18 See *Marchant v Capital & Counties Plc* [1983] 2 EGLR 156.

19 See 1939 Act, s 55(n)(i); 1894 Act, s 91(1).

the adjoining owner who received the notice, and until the operations involved in the notice are concluded'.[20]

It is not thought, however, that the removal of the key reference to settling matters 'from time to time' has deprived the surveyors of their power to make successive awards as separate issues arise. This power is not only useful, it is an essential feature of the procedure under the Act. While the principal issue is always likely to be what work can be done, and how, the Act itself provides for quite separate matters to be determined under s 10[21] which can conveniently, and in some cases can only,[22] be dealt with by separate awards. It is considered that this framework is enough to demonstrate that the surveyors can make a succession of awards, determining different issues, as necessary.

8.15 MULTIPLE PARTIES

The complexities of the procedure under s 10 are compounded if there is more than one adjoining owner. There is no right to require all adjoining owners to appoint the same surveyor, and no procedure for consolidating disputes which are being adjudicated by different surveyors. Nor can an award against one adjoining owner create any estoppel against another. Thus the building owner is faced with the possibility of inconsistent awards leading to paralysis. If all adjoining owners do appoint the same surveyor, it should be possible to minimise this risk by arrangements equivalent to consolidation. Alternatively, if the same third surveyor is selected in each case, he can be called on (under s 10(11)) to make all the awards.

8.16 PROCEDURE AND FORM OF AWARD

The surveyors are not arbitrators,[23] and do not have the benefit of the procedural powers conferred on arbitrators by the Arbitration Acts. They are not bound to hold a hearing at which the views of the parties can be put forward. Their duty was described in Parliament as '... quasi-arbitral. Once appointed they have a duty to act properly in the interests of both parties as statutory surveyors, which is a most important safeguard'.[24] Their award should deal with the matters mentioned in s 10(12) and (13)'[25] It is also usual for it to make detailed provisions for matters required by s 7, for example measures designed to minimise inconvenience to adjoining owners and occupiers. An award is to be given a reasonably benevolent construction 'without pedantic

---

20 See *Selby v Whitbread & Co* [1917] 1 KB 736 at 742.
21 For example security under s 12.
22 For example objections to an account under s 13(2).
23 See para **8.17**.
24 See Hansard HL Debates, Vol 568, 31 Jan 1996, Col 1538.
25 See para **8.12**.

strictness or meticulous severity'.[26] A specimen form of award is included in Appendix 4.

8.17   SURVEYORS AS ARBITRATORS

It is considered that the Arbitration Acts do not apply to the surveyors, although the authorities are not altogether consistent.

There are a number of earlier authorities which speak of the surveyors as arbitrators,[27] but only one (decided at first instance upon the Metropolitan Building Act 1855) which has actually held that they are subject to the provisions of the Arbitration Acts.[28]

More recently, it has been held that the Arbitration Acts are 'plainly' excluded by what is now s 10(16), which provides that the award is conclusive.[29] In the light of ss 94–97 of the Arbitration Act 1996 (formerly Arbitration Act 1950, s 31), this conclusion is not quite so plain, since s 94 of that Act applies the arbitration legislation (with modifications) to 'statutory arbitrations' except so far as this produces inconsistency. It is nevertheless submitted that the conclusion remains correct. The procedure under s 10 is a self-contained code, designed to work informally and expeditiously. It is more akin to a determination by experts than to arbitration.[30] The expression 'statutory arbitration' should be reserved for procedures expressly described as arbitration in their parent statutes,[31] which are intended to take advantage of the arbitration machinery.

8.18   IMMUNITY OF SURVEYORS

The question arises whether the surveyors are vulnerable to claims in negligence by the parties, or enjoy quasi-judicial immunity. It is difficult to provide a confident answer. The leading authorities are the decisions of the House of Lords in *Sutcliffe v Thackrah*[32] and *Arenson v Casson Beckman Rutley & Co*[33] ('*Sutcliffe*' and '*Arenson*').

---

26 See *Selby v Whitbread & Co* [1917] 1 KB 736 at 744.
27 Notably *Re Stone and Hastie* [1903] 2 KB 463, where a procedure under the Arbitration Act 1889 was followed, but its applicability was assumed, not decided; *Leadbetter v Marylebone Corp* [1904] 2 KB 893, CA; *Selby v Whitbread & Co* [1917] 1 KB 736; *Burlington Property Co Ltd v Odeon Theatres Ltd* [1939] 1 KB 633.
28 *Re Metropolitan Building Act, ex parte McBryde* (1876) 4 Ch D 200.
29 See *Chartered Society of Physiotherapy v Simmonds Church Smiles* [1995] 1 EGLR 155.
30 Ibid.
31 For example Agricultural Tenancies Act 1995, s 28.
32 [1974] AC 727.
33 [1977] AC 405.

The general principle is not that people who decide differences or disputes between rival parties are immune because they have to act fairly, but that they owe a duty of care to the parties, and any immunity is exceptional (see *Arenson*). Thus the surveyors will owe a duty of care to both parties.

In *Sutcliffe* it was assumed that arbitrators enjoyed an immunity, which extended also to 'quasi-arbitrators'.[34] But in *Arenson* so much doubt was cast on the arbitrator's immunity[35] that arbitrators have now been expressly protected by statute.[36] If it is correct that the surveyors are not arbitrators,[37] this will not assist them.

Thus the question is whether the surveyors are immune as quasi-arbitrators. They satisfy the most important criterion identified in *Arenson*, ie they determine formulated disputes. On the other hand, their procedure has been characterised as in the nature of an expert determination,[38] and experts are not normally immune, particularly if they are entitled to act solely on their own opinion, rather than upon evidence presented to them.[39]

In this state of the authorities, any prudent surveyor will wish to make sure that his insurance covers his activities under the Act. He may also wish to consider stipulating for immunity.

---

34 See esp per Lord Morris at p 752–753.
35 See eg per Lord Kilbrandon at p 431.
36 See Arbitration Act 1996, s 29(1).
37 See para **8.17**.
38 See para **8.17**.
39 See *Palacath Ltd v Flanagan* [1985] 2 All ER 161.

Chapter 9

THE AWARD – EFFECT AND ENFORCEMENT

9.1 INTRODUCTION

The procedure leading to an award, and the scope of the award and the surveyors' jurisdiction, are considered in Chapter 8. The procedures for upsetting an award by appeal or for excess of jurisdiction are considered in Chapter 10. This chapter is concerned with the effect of an award and its enforcement.

9.2 EFFECT

A valid award which is not appealed, conclusively determines the dispute which had arisen, or had been deemed to arise, under the Act, and it cannot be questioned in any court (s 10(16)). This has the following consequences.

(a) The building owner can carry out the works authorised by the award, even though they infringe the adjoining owner's rights at common law.

(b) The authorised works become works 'in pursuance of this Act', so that the rights of entry for the purpose of executing them become exercisable (s 8(1)), and must be respected by the adjoining owner, on pain of criminal liability (under s 16).

(c) Both parties must observe the terms of the award, and each will be able to enforce them against the other. The building owner must carry out all works directed for the convenience or protection of the adjoining owner. If the adjoining owner is ordered to pay a contribution to expenses, then (subject to due service of an account under s 13) he must do so.

(d) Adjoining occupiers are also affected. They have no right of appeal, and can only resist an award if they can show that it was made without jurisdiction. Subject to that, they too must observe the rights of entry, and rely on ss 7(1), (2) and (3) for any redress.[1]

9.3 ESTOPPEL

A judgment of a competent court creates an estoppel by record, which prevents the parties and their successors from reopening the same cause of action. It also creates issue estoppel, which prevents them later raising issues which were

---

1 See Chapter 6.

raised, or could have been raised, in the earlier proceedings.[2] By extension, these doctrines apply also to arbitration awards and the decisions of all kinds of domestic tribunals.[3] In principle, therefore, an award under the Act appears to be capable of creating both cause of action estoppel and issue estoppel between the parties.

The nature of the issues settled by an award leaves relatively little scope for the operation of estoppel. For example, an award may, without addressing any issue of law, direct that certain work can be done within a certain time. If the time expires without a start being made, the building owner may serve a fresh notice proposing the same work. The fact that time has passed, and circumstances may have changed, probably means that neither party is effectively estopped from advancing the same factual arguments as before.

Further, a tribunal of limited jurisdiction cannot by its own decision enlarge or diminish its jurisdiction, so that its decisions on its own jurisdiction create no estoppel.[4] Thus a decision by the surveyors that, for example, some structure is a party structure will create no estoppel if they would not otherwise have had jurisdiction.

It may nevertheless be that an award involves decisions capable of creating estoppel. For example the surveyors may have to decide whether a right to light exists before deciding what work can be carried out.[5] This may go not to jurisdiction, but merely to the manner of its exercise.

9.4 ENFORCEMENT

Since the better view is that the procedure under s 10 is not an arbitration,[6] it follows that an award is not capable of being enforced under s 66 of the Arbitration Act 1996. If the terms of an award are not observed, therefore, the remedy of the aggrieved party is to bring an action on the award. The procedures available vary according to the nature of the term which is breached and the remedy which is desired. The term may be one which directs: (a) the payment of money; or (b) the doing (or refraining from doing) of some act; and in respect of (b) the remedy desired may be damages or specific relief. These possibilities will be considered in turn.

---

2 See *Halsbury's Laws*, 4th edn, Vol 16, paras 974–982.
3 See ibid, paras 1012–1016: estoppel quasi by record.
4 See *Crown Estate Commissioners v Dorset County Council* [1990] Ch 297.
5 See para **15.4**.
6 See para **8.17**.

9.5 PAYMENT OF MONEY

There are two procedures for recovering sums of money which an award directs to be paid.

(a) Any sum payable in pursuance of the Act (other than a fine) is recoverable summarily as a civil debt.[7] This summary procedure is by way of complaint to the magistrates' court, and is governed by the Magistrates' Court Act 1980.[8] The magistrates' court has power to award costs;[9] payment may be enforced by distress warrant;[10] there is no power to impose a sentence of imprisonment in default of payment.[11]

(b) Section 17 does not provide that the summary procedure is to be the only way of recovering money payable in pursuance of the Act. It therefore leaves unimpaired the county court's jurisdiction to try actions for sums recoverable by virtue of any enactment.[12] Since sums directed to be paid by an award are recoverable by virtue of the Act, a civil action in the county court for payment is available as an alternative.

9.6 BREACH OF TERM

An award may impose positive or negative obligations on one party, for breach of which the other party may wish to claim either damages or specific relief. It is not altogether clear what is the nature of this cause of action. It cannot be breach of contract, since an award is not, and is nowhere deemed to be, a contract. It is considered that it is implicit in s 10 that both parties are under a statutory duty to observe the terms of an award, so that the cause of action is breach of statutory duty. The duty is not a public duty, which might be enforceable only by the Attorney-General, but a private duty owed by the parties to each other. And since the Act provides no remedy for its breach, there is no difficulty in concluding that the parties are entitled to enforce it against each other. As Lord Simonds said:

> '... if a statutory duty is prescribed but no remedy by way of penalty or otherwise is imposed, it can be assumed that a right of civil action accrues to the person who is damnified by the breach. For, if it were not so, the statute would be but a pious aspiration.[13]'

---

7 See s 17.
8 Section 58.
9 Ibid, s 64.
10 Ibid, s 76.
11 Ibid, s 92.
12 Under the County Courts Act 1984, s 16.
13 See *Cutler v Wandsworth Stadium Ltd* [1949] AC 398, at p 407; *Thornton v Kirklees Metropolitan Borough Council* [1979] 2 All ER 349, CA.

9.7　DAMAGES

In principle, therefore, the aggrieved party can claim damages for breach of the terms of an award.[14] In this connection the following points may be mentioned.

(a)　Since breach of statutory duty is a tort,[15] the measure of damages is the tortious measure. The classic formulation is that of Lord Blackburn:

'...the sum of money which will put the party who has been injured ... in the same position as he would have been in if he had not sustained the wrong...'[16]

(b)　It is likely that the breach will consist of failure by the building owner to provide some work intended to benefit the adjoining owner, or failure to provide it to an adequate standard. This is a notoriously difficult area for the assessment of damages, since the cost of carrying out the necessary work often exceeds the diminution in value of the plaintiff's property. In such a case, the plaintiff will normally recover the cost of the work only if he genuinely intends to carry it out.[17]

(c)　Such costs will normally be assessed at the date of the hearing, but might be assessed at an earlier date if the plaintiff ought reasonably to have done the work earlier.[18]

(d)　If the diminution in value is nil, and the cost of reinstatement disproportionate, the court may award a modest sum for loss of amenity.[19]

9.8　SPECIFIC RELIEF

Specific performance (the usual form of specific relief) is a remedy available only in contract. But an injunction can be granted to restrain a breach of statutory duty, and a suitably framed mandatory injunction will have the same effect as an order for specific performance.[20] Historically, the court has been reluctant to enforce specifically an obligation to build, but it is not clear how far this attitude would affect a claim for breach of statutory duty. In any event, the court is nowadays prepared to order specific performance where the works are sufficiently defined,[21] and this requirement ought to be supplied by the compulsory plans (under s 7(5)).

14　As happened in *Selby v Whitbread & Co* [1917] 1 KB 736.

15　See *Thornton v Kirklees Metropolitan Borough Council* [1979] 2 All ER 349, CA.

16　See *Livingstone v Rawyards Coal Co* (1880) 5 App Cas 25, at p 39.

17　See *Ward v Cannock Chase District Council* [1986] Ch 546.

18　See *Dodd Properties (Kent) Ltd v Canterbury City Council* [1980] 1 All ER 928.

19　See *Ruxley Electronics and Construction Ltd v Forsyth* [1995] 3 All ER 268, which, however, is a contract case.

20　See *Warder v Cooper* [1970] 1 Ch 495, where a mandatory injunction (ordering possession) was granted as well as a negative injunction.

21　See *Jeune v Queen's Cross Properties Ltd* [1974] Ch 97.

9.9 ACTION OUTSIDE THE AWARD

If the award contains detailed provisions giving effect to all the adjoining owner's rights, including those under s 7(1), (2) and (3), there should be no reason for him to bring any action outside the award. Any infringement of his rights will be a breach of some term in the award, and will give rise to an action on the award. But if the award is not so detailed, and some infringement of his rights occurs which is not also a breach of some term in the award, he will be able to bring a separate claim for breach of the statutory duty in question. It is clear that those sections, no less than the award, give rise to statutory duties which he can enforce personally.[22] So far as adjoining occupiers are concerned, this is the only form of redress which is likely to be open to them, since the award will not normally contain terms for their direct benefit.

9.10 INTEREST

Courts have power to award interest on any debt or damages.[23] Interest accrues automatically on judgment debts at a prescribed rate, which is varied from time to time by statutory instrument.[24] Arbitrators can award interest.[25] These are all statutory powers: there is no power to award interest at common law.[26] Since the Act nowhere mentions interest it is clear that the surveyors cannot include any provision for interest in the award.

9.11 VENUE

The High Court has jurisdiction over all the causes of action which have been discussed.[27] The county court's jurisdiction in respect of claims for payment has been mentioned at para **9.5**(b). The county court also has unlimited jurisdiction over actions in tort,[28] and this includes actions for breach of statutory duty.[29] There is therefore a choice between the High Court and the county court, which should be governed principally by the High Court and County Courts Jurisdiction Order 1991. This sets out in art 7(5) the criteria for transferring actions from the county court to the High Court. These include:

(a) the financial substance of the action;

---

22 See para **9.6**.
23 See Supreme Court Act 1981, s 35A; County Courts Act 1984, s 69.
24 Judgments Act 1838, s 17; County Courts Act 1984, s 74.
25 Arbitration Act 1996, s 49.
26 See *London Chatham & Dover Railway Co v South Eastern Railway Co* [1893] AC 429, HL; *President of India v La Pintada Compania Navigacion SA* [1985] AC 104.
27 Except the summary procedure under s 17.
28 See County Courts Act 1984, s 15(1).
29 See *Thornton v Kirklees Metropolitan Borough Council* [1979] 2 All ER 349, CA.

(b) whether the action is otherwise important;

(c) the complexity of the facts, legal issues or remedies or procedures involved; and

(d) whether transfer is likely to result in a more speedy trial of the action.

Prima facie, an appeal with a value of less than £25,000 is to be tried in the county court, under Art 7(3). This means one where the appellant could reasonably state the financial worth of the appeal to him as being £25,000 or less.[30] Cases with a value of £50,000 or more are normally to be tried in the High Court. Thus in deciding whether to transfer, the court would in the first instance have to consider the value of the action. If it is more than £50,000, it ought prima facie to be heard in the High Court, and if it is below £25,000, it ought prima facie to be heard in the county court. It is then necessary to consider the criteria set out above. Given the technical complexity of the issues likely to arise on an appeal, consideration should be given in many cases to transferring the appeal to an Official Referee[31].

9.12 LIMITATION

The application of the Limitation Act 1980 to the causes of action which have been discussed raises difficult questions. Reference should be made to specialised works on limitation.[32] However, some general points may be made here.

There are several competing sections of the 1980 Act which may be applicable.

(a) Section 2 provides a 6-year period for actions in tort. Whether an action for breach of statutory duty is an action founded on tort for limitation purposes is doubtful. A purely statutory cause of action has been assumed in the House of Lords to be governed by this section.[33]

(b) Section 7 provides a 6-year period for actions 'to enforce an award, where the submission is not by an instrument under seal'. In s 34, 'award' is defined in terms of arbitration, but that definition does not apply to s 7. It probably does not apply to the surveyors' award, which does not result from any submission.

(c) Section 9 provides a 6-year period for actions to recover 'any sum recoverable by virtue of any enactment'. Fine distinctions have been drawn under this section and its predecessor,[34] but it is thought that it probably applies to liquidated and unliquidated sums whether due under an award

---

30 See Art 9(1)(b)(i).
31 As was done in *Chartered Society of Physiotherapy v Simmonds Church Smiles* [1995] 1 EGLR 155.
32 For example McGee, *Limitation Periods* (Sweet & Maxwell, 1994).
33 See *Sevcon Ltd v Lucas CAV Ltd* [1986] 2 All ER 104.
34 See McGee, op cit, pp 49ff, 184ff.

or outside an award (eg under s 7(2)). But it does not apply to claims for specific relief by injunction.

(d) Section 8 provides a 12-year period for actions 'upon a speciality', unless a shorter period is prescribed elsewhere. A statute is a speciality. This section does not extend the 6-year period where ss 2 or 9 apply, but may be applicable (by analogy) to claims to specific relief by injunction.[35]

(e) Section 36 provides that the time-limits under ss 2, 7, 8 and 9 do not apply to claims for an injunction or other equitable relief, except by analogy. but the equitable doctrines of laches and acquiescence do apply.

The date of accrual of a cause of action under a statute often gives rise to difficulty,[36] but it is not thought that causes of action under the Act will raise serious doubts. The cause of action on an award will accrue when there is a breach of any term of the award.[37] The direct causes of action under s 7 will accrue when the breach of duty occurs (under s 7(1) or (3)), or the work is done which causes the loss or damage (s 7(2)).

---

35 See *Collin v Duke of Westminster* [1985] QB 581.
36 See eg *Yorkshire Electricity Board v British Telecom* [1986] 2 All ER 961.
37 Compare *Agromet Motoimport Ltd v Maulden Engineering Co (Beds) Ltd* [1985] 2 All ER 436.

Chapter 10

RIGHTS OF APPEAL

10.1 INTRODUCTION

Section 10(17) of the Act provides that:

'Either of the parties to the dispute may, within the period of fourteen days beginning with the day on which an award made under this section is served upon him, appeal to the county court against the award and the county court may—

(a) rescind the award or modify it in such manner as the court thinks fit; and

(b) make such order as to costs as the court thinks fit.'

This provision re-enacts s 55(n)(i) of the 1939 Act. Section 55(n)(ii) and (o) of the 1939 Act, concerned with appeals to the High Court, are not repeated in the Act.

The scheme of the Act is to provide a statutory right of appeal from any award by the surveyors. The right of appeal arises in the case of all awards, and therefore covers awards by an agreed surveyor, awards by any two of the three surveyors, and awards by the third surveyor alone.[1]

Section 10(16) provides that (subject to any appeal) 'The award shall be conclusive and shall not except as provided by this section be questioned in any court'.

10.2 EXTENT OF MATTERS WHICH CAN BE RAISED ON APPEAL

The wording of s 10(17) is wide and general, and suggests that the court has complete discretion as to what order to make. It removes the comparison between the dual procedures for appeal under s 55(n) and (o) of the 1939 Act.

In relation to appeals from the High Court or a county court to the Court of Appeal, there are in practice limits to the functions of review which the Court of Appeal will exercise. The most important of these limitations are that the Court of Appeal:

(a) does not retry the case in the sense of hearing all the evidence adduced before the court below;

(b) will not in general receive fresh evidence itself, which was not before the court below;

---

1 See s 10(10) and (11).

(c) will not in general allow a case to be made which was not made in the court
     below;

(d) will only reverse the finding of the court below on a question of fact if it is
     clearly shown that the decision is wrong, particularly where the decision
     depended on the credibility as assessed by the lower court of witnesses;

(e) will only interfere with the exercise of a discretion by the court below if the
     decision of the court below was totally unreasonable or made under a
     mistake of law.

These principles are summarised in the notes to Ord 59 of the Rules of the
Supreme Court 1965 in Vol 1 of *The Supreme Court Practice 1996*.

If the county court were to apply these principles, the right of appeal against the
surveyors' award would be much less extensive than a complete review. In
favour of such a view, there are the following arguments:

(a) the county court is inherently ill-equipped to rehear disputes involving
     potentially considerable amounts of technical and expert material;

(b) unless there is a strict limit on the matters that can be ventilated on
     appeal, considerable uncertainty and expense will result, possibly
     disproportionate to the matters in dispute;

(c) there is an analogy in the case of architect's certificates issued under
     building contracts. The court has no power to reopen such certificates,[2]
     but retains the right to intervene where the certifier has failed to act
     lawfully and fairly.[3]

On the other hand, the arguments in favour of the court having a wider power
of review are:

(a) the statute places no express limitation on the court's power;

(b) the analogy of architect's certificates is not apt. In the case of architect's
     certificates, the parties have agreed by contract to be bound by these,
     subject to an arbitrator's power of review. By contrast, the rights and duties
     created by the Act do not arise from contract;

(c) the surveyors are not obliged to act judicially or in any set procedural way.
     There is therefore good reason for allowing the court to review their
     decision.

The county court deals with various appeals under other provisions. In *British
and Argentine Meat Co Ltd v Randall*,[4] a statutory provision provided for

---

2 *Northern Regional Health Authority v Derek Crouch Construction Co Ltd* [1984] 2 All ER 175, CA.
3 *University of Reading v Miller Construction* (1995) 75 BLR 91; *John Barker Construction Ltd v
   London Portman Hotel Ltd* [1995] CILL 1152.
4 [1939] 4 All ER 293, CA.

reference to a referee for inquiry and report, and empowered the judge 'on consideration of any report or further report [to] give such judgment or make such order in the action or matter as may be just, without prejudice to any right of appeal'. It was held that under this provision, the decision was one for the judge alone, that he was free to accept or reject the referee's report, and that he ought to receive fresh evidence if tendered to him. On the other hand, where a county court judge is hearing an appeal from a district judge the position is different. Order 39, r 6 of the County Court Rules 1981, empowers the judge to set aside or vary the judgment or order of the district judge and to give any other judgment or make any other order in substitution. But where the judge hears an appeal from a decision of the district judge, he cannot interfere with the district judge's decision (except in an interlocutory matter) unless he considers that no reasonable district judge could have exercised his discretion in the way that was done.[5]

The only decided case, on the provisions of the 1939 Act is *Chartered Society of Physiotherapy v Simmonds Church Smiles*.[6] In that case, it was held that in relation to an appeal to the county court (which was in fact transferred to the High Court under s 42 of the County Courts Act 1984) the court had full power to reopen the award. The Official Referee said:[7]

'Looking at the whole of section 55(n) and (o) it is, in my judgment, clear that the award is one which may be completely reopened if an appeal is duly made. Section 55(n)(i) [corresponding to s 10(17) of the Act] provides that the county court may "... modify it in such manner and make such order as to costs as it thinks fit." In my view the words "as it thinks fit" plainly qualify "modify in such manner" and are not limited to an "order as to costs", for otherwise "such manner" is left hanging in the air [the wording of s 10(17) of the Act, which provides separately for modification of the award and costs in sub-paragraphs (a) and (b) now clarifies this point]. Thus the Court has in my judgment, wide powers to alter any award and to do so must have the power to substitute its own finding or conclusion for any finding or conclusion that the surveyor(s) made or may be presumed to have made.'

The Official Referee rejected an argument that the court had no power to receive further evidence. He took the view that the court's powers were not circumscribed by the 1939 Act, and that it was open to the court to receive fresh evidence (including expert evidence) in relation to the issues which were subject to appeal.

The Act post-dates this decision, and in the Parliamentary Debates it was said that 'the aims of the Bill are to extend the tried and tested provisions of the London Building Acts to England and Wales'.[8] 'The intention remains, as always, that the Bill will follow as closely as possible the London Building Acts

---

5 *Woodspring District Council v Taylor* (1982) 133 NLJ 556, CA.
6 [1995] 1 EGLR 155.
7 [1995] 1 EGLR 157H.
8 Hansard HL Debates, Vol 568, No 35, 31 Jan 1996, Col 1536.

which are its role model and the precedents and practice which have been established for Inner London over a long period of time'.[9]

In the circumstances, it appears that Parliament may be taken to have intended to approve the decision in the *Chartered Society of Physiotherapy* case.[10] The point could be raised again before an appellate court, but it is submitted that the case was correctly decided, notwithstanding the practical difficulties to which it gives rise. The key consideration is the fact that the surveyors are under no obligation to act judicially. Since they are, therefore, under no formal obligation to hear both parties, and may make use of their own expertise, there is no effective way of the court reviewing their decision without itself rehearing the whole matter, or so much of it as is necessary to determine the points in issue.

10.3   MODE OF APPEAL

The procedure for appeal is laid down by Ord 3, r 6 of the County Court Rules 1981. Order 3, r 6(2) provides that the appellant is within 21 days after the date of the award to file a request for the entry of the appeal and a copy of the award appealed against. The form for Request for Entry of Appeal[11] requires that the award be annexed, and the grounds of appeal included. The court should, it is submitted, normally fix as the return day a day for pre-trial review, at which directions should be given for the further conduct of the appeal, including:

(a)   exchange of any further pleadings (eg a cross-appeal by the respondent, or a summary of the arguments advanced by the respondent in support of the award);

(b)   exchange of witness statements and expert evidence proofs;

(c)   discovery;

(d)   directions for trial of the appeal.

10.4   APPEAL TO THE COURT OF APPEAL

Article 2(1)(b) of the County Courts Appeals Order 1991, requires that leave to appeal be obtained either from a judge of the county court or from the Court of Appeal where the decision reached is one by the judge acting in an appellate capacity. It is submitted, tentatively, that in the light of the *Chartered Society of Physiotherapy* case the decision of the court on an appeal under s 10 of the Act would not be one by the judge sitting in an appellate capacity, because the definition in the order only refers to a judge hearing an appeal against or

---

9 Hansard HL Debates, Vol 572, No 96, 22 May 1996, Col 931.
10 See *EWP Limited v Moore* [1991] 2 EGLR 4, CA.
11 County Court Practice Form N209: see Appendix 4 Precedent 13.

application in respect of a judicial decision.[12] As the Official Referee pointed out in the *Chartered Society of Physiotherapy* case, the proceedings by the surveyors are not in truth judicial proceedings, so that the decision of the court is in effect the first judicial consideration of the matters in issue. If this is right, there is a right of appeal to the Court of Appeal under s 77 of the County Courts Act 1984. Procedure on appeal is governed by Ord 59 of the Rules of the Supreme Court 1965, and reference should be made to the text of this.[13]

10.5 TIME-LIMITS

Section 10(17) lays down a 14-day time-limit for an appeal, running from the date of service of the award. Section 15 of the Act regulates service. It is submitted that the 14-day time-limit is mandatory and, subject as set out below, incapable of extension either by the surveyors or the court, so that failure to enter an appeal in time results in the right of appeal being lost. The general rule is that where a time-limit is laid down by statute, it cannot be extended either by the court or by agreement.[14] The statutory period includes any bank holidays occurring within it.[15] Where the appellant has done everything required of him, his appeal will be 'made' when received at the court office even though the court delays in issuing the process.[16] If the last day for making the appeal falls on a day when the court office is closed the application may be filed on the next day it is open.[17]

10.6 EFFECT OF APPEAL

The Act is silent on the question whether, pending appeal, the award binds the parties, or whether it is in effect suspended, so that neither party can act on it. Principle strongly favours the latter solution, at any rate in relation to those parts of the award subject to appeal, because once work has been done it may be impractical or very expensive to undo. If therefore an appeal is successful, the position of both building and adjoining owner may be unsatisfactory. It is submitted that the effect of the machinery for appeal laid down by the Act is that the award is suspended by appeal; this is supported by the following:

---

12 See *The Supreme Court Practice 1997* Vol 1, pp 942–943.
13 Set out in *The Supreme Court Practice 1997*, and the notes thereto.
14 *Hodgson v Armstrong* [1967] 1 All ER 307, CA; *Kammin's Ballrooms Co Ltd v Zenith Investments (Torquay) Ltd* [1970] 2 All ER 871, HL; *Smith v East Elloe Rural District Council* [1956] AC 736.
15 Compare *Stainer v Secretary of State for the Environment and Shepway District Council* [1993] EGCS 130.
16 *Aly v Aly* (1984) 128 SJ 65.
17 Compare *Hodgson v Armstrong* [1967] 1 All ER 307, CA.

(a) Section 10(16) refers to the position where the award is not appealed. By implication, the award will *not* be 'conclusive' if it *is* appealed.

(b) The wide power of review given to the court is inconsistent with the parties' rights being fixed until an appeal is heard.

(c) The short time-limit for appeal suggests some urgency, more consistent with suspension of action until the appeal is decided.[18]

10.7   OTHER METHODS OF CHALLENGING AN AWARD

It is considered that an award could not be challenged by way of judicial review. The words of the Act purporting to make an award conclusive are probably not enough to preclude judicial review.[19] But a dispute regarding an award is concerned solely with private rights, and in the absence of any public law element no question could arise of judicial review.[20] A further obstacle to judicial review would lie in the existence of an alternative remedy by way of appeal.[21]

An award which is ultra vires may be challenged on that ground, notwithstanding that it has not been appealed.[22]

10.8   SEVERABILITY

The fact that the award is invalid in part will not invalidate the whole award, provided the invalid part is severable, and not 'inextricably connected' with the remainder.[23] In applying this test the court would have to have regard to two questions.

(a) Whether the void part of the award is capable of being excised without substantially affecting the sense and grammar of the remainder of the award.[24]

---

18 Support for this view can be found in *Standard Bank of British South America v Stokes* (1878) 9 Ch D 68 at 77, although the specific point there considered was whether the award took effect before the decision of the third surveyor.

19 See for example *Anisminic v Foreign Compensation Commission* [1967] 2 All ER 986, CA; *Pearlman v Keepers and Governors of Harrow School* [1979] 1 All ER 365.

20 Compare *R v Chief Rabbi of the United Hebrew Congregations of Great Britain and the Commonwealth* [1993] 2 All ER 249.

21 Compare *R v Birmingham City Council ex parte Ferrero Ltd* [1993] 1 All ER 530, CA.

22 See *Re Stone and Hastie* [1903] 2 KB 463; *Gyle-Thompson v Wall Street Properties Ltd* [1974] 1 All ER 295; *Woodhouse v Consolidated Property Corp* [1993] 1 EGLR 174, CA.

23 *Selby v Whitbread & Co* [1917] 1 KB 736 at 748.

24 Compare *T Lucas & Co Ltd v Mitchell* [1974] Ch 129, a case on an invalid restraint of trade.

(b) Whether the excision of the invalid part radically alters the nature of the remainder of the obligations in question, or the award as a whole.[25] If the void part of the award cannot be removed without fundamentally altering its effect, or without substantially rewriting it, the whole award will be invalid.

---

25 Compare *Amoco Australia Pty Ltd v Rocca Bros Motor Engineering Co Pty Ltd* [1975] AC 561.

Chapter 11

FINANCIAL MATTERS

11.1 INTRODUCTION

Work carried out in pursuance of the Act has a financial impact in three areas. First, there is the cost of the work carried out by a building owner pursuant to an award under the Act. Secondly, there are the costs involved in operating the dispute resolution procedure under the Act, including such matters as the fees of the surveyors and costs incurred by the parties in relation to an award. Thirdly, the Act envisages contingent liabilities which may arise in the future, for example where the adjoining owner makes greater use of the works than anticipated. The provisions are of great importance in practice, and need to be carefully scrutinised by building and adjoining owners and their advisers when any work to which the Act applies is under consideration.

11.2 THE MEANING OF 'COSTS' AND 'EXPENSES'

Confusion can result if the terminology used by the Act is not appreciated. The Act distinguishes between 'costs' and 'expenses', but without defining either term.

11.2.1 Costs

Costs are mentioned several times in s 10 in contexts which make it clear that the term means much the same as it does when used in relation to litigation.[1] Thus, it will include:

(a) the fees of any surveyor appointed to discharge functions under the Act; and

(b) legal and other professional costs incurred by the parties in relation to operating the procedures of the Act.

These costs would include, for example, those incurred in relation to service of notices, fees of engineering and other consultants, and fees for legal advice related to the procedures of the Act. Although the machinery for making an award does not prescribe a formal hearing by the surveyors, the possibility of an informal hearing is clearly envisaged by the Act. For example in *Chartered Society of Physiotherapy v Simmonds Church Smiles*,[2] the parties' surveyors having disagreed, the third surveyor held a hearing at which he was addressed by the

---

1 See s 10(12), (13), (15), (17).
2 [1995] 1 EGLR 155.

parties' surveyors, and subsequently made his award. The costs of such a hearing would qualify as 'costs'.

11.2.2 Expenses

The terms 'expense' and 'expenses' occur frequently in the Act (ss 1(3)(b), 1(4)(a), 1(7), 11, 12, 13, 14). It is clear that they refer to the actual cost of carrying out work. Presumably (although this is not spelt out in the Act), expenses would include not only the prime cost of work but also reasonable incidental professional fees, fees paid to statutory authorities, and insurance related to the work.

Where, as often happens, work to which the Act applies is carried out as part of a wider project, it is presumably necessary to separate out the expenses relating to the work to which the Act applies from the global cost of the project. In the case of the prime cost of the work, this exercise may be straightforward, simply extracting the relevant elements from the bills of quantities or specification. But there may be arguments as to the apportionment of preliminaries, for example whether they should be apportioned directly proportional to the cost of the relevant work, or in some other way, if for example a large element of the preliminaries is directly related to the need to provide temporary protection and support to the party wall. No doubt the surveyors will have to consider what is fair and reasonable in the circumstances.

Costs of matters too remote from the work will not fall within the definition of expenses. This would exclude feasibility studies, environmental assessments, and costs related to the obtaining of planning permission.

11.3   EXPENSES: GENERAL RULE

The general rule is that except as provided under s 11, expenses of work under the Act are to be defrayed by the building owner (s 11(1)). Section 11 then sets out a number of cases where the general rule is not to apply. These include a number of contingent liabilities, which may occur some time in the future, which are considered more fully in Chapter 14.

In addition to the general rule of s 11(1), reference should be made to the following provisions of the Act which expressly cast liability for expenses on the building owner.

(a)   Section 1(4), where the adjoining owner does not consent to the building of a party wall or party fence wall.

(b)   Section 1(7), where the building owner desires to build on the line of junction a wall placed wholly on his own land.

(c) Section 6(3), where the building owner bears the expense of underpinning or otherwise strengthening or safeguarding the foundations of the building or structure of the adjoining owner.

11.4 LIABILITIES OF ADJOINING OWNER

There is a medley of separate provisions, the unifying theme of which is that where the expense in question confers a benefit on the adjoining owner, or is incurred at his request, he ought to bear part of it. However, only certain cases are covered, and there is no general principle that wherever work benefits an adjoining owner (eg by improving the stability or fabric of his building) he is automatically liable to contribute to the expense. The circumstances where the adjoining owner may be called upon to contribute to the expenses are as follows.

11.4.1 Section 11(3)

Where a new party wall is constructed with the agreement of the adjoining owner, ss 1(3)(b) and 11(3) require the expense to be apportioned having regard to the use made or to be made of the wall by each of the building and adjoining owner respectively and to the cost of labour and materials prevailing at the time when that use is made by each. Thus, for example, if a party wall is built which is an external wall of the building owner's building, and the adjoining owner derives no benefit from it except in its function as a boundary wall, the building owner will be obliged to bear the majority of the expenses at that time. If the adjoining owner later constructs a building of his own against the wall, thus making greater use of it, he will become liable to a 'clawback' by the building owner, representing a fair contribution in respect of his increased use of the wall. The clawback will reflect costs current at the time the adjoining owner constructs his building, not costs actually incurred by the building owner when the wall was built originally.

11.4.2 Section 11(4)

Where work of underpinning, thickening or raising a party structure, party fence wall or an external wall which belongs to the building owner and is built against a party structure or party fence wall, is necessitated by a defect or want of repair of the structure or wall concerned, ss 2(2)(a) and 11(4) enable the building owner to recoup expenses which result from him having to repair the party structure as opposed to carrying out work to his own specification. The expenses have to be apportioned, and the factors to be taken into account are the use by each owner and the responsibility for the defect or want of repair concerned, if more than one owner makes use of the structure or wall concerned (s 11(4)). The concept of responsibility here appears to be related to the use made of the wall by the parties rather than any legal liability for repair. In other words, the question seems to be not so much which owner is legally responsible but which owner's use has contributed more to the disrepair.

11.4.3   Section 11(5)

Where work is carried out to make good, repair or demolish and rebuild a party structure or party fence wall, in a case where such work is necessitated by a defect or want of repair of the structure or wall, ss 2(2)(b) and 11(5) require an apportionment of the same kind as under s 11(4).

11.4.4   Section 11(7)

Where the building owner wishes to reduce the height of a party (fence) wall under s 2(2)(m), and the adjoining owner serves a counter-notice requiring the existing height of the wall to be maintained, s 11(7) requires the adjoining owner to bear a due proportion of the cost of the wall so far as it exceeds 6 metres in height, or the height currently enclosed upon by his own building.

11.4.5   Section 11(9)

Where the adjoining owner requests or requires work to be done, and it is carried out by the building owner, s 11(9) provides that the adjoining owner must pay for what he has requested or required. A request could presumably be made at any time before the work is carried out: a requirement would be by counter-notice under s 4. But if the adjoining owner requires underpinning under s 6(3), that section requires the building owner to pay, and overrides s 11(9).

11.4.6   Section 11(11)

Where use is subsequently made by the adjoining owner of work carried out solely at the expense of the building owner, s 11(11) provides for a clawback payment to the building owner, representing a due proportion of the expense. As under s 11(3), the apportionment is assessed by reference to current values at the time when the adjoining owner makes use of the work.

11.5   COSTS

Costs are within the surveyors' discretion.[3] No principles are prescribed upon which they should be awarded, but the usual form of award requires the building owner to pay the adjoining owner's surveyor's fees in connection with the award and the inspection of the works.[4] This seems consistent with the

---

3 See s 10(13).
4 See Appendix 4 for a precedent award.

general principle that the building owner, for whose benefit the work is being carried out, should bear the costs, except where there is a specific provision to the contrary.

In normal arbitration, the practice is that the successful party receives his costs, except where a substantial part of the time and costs of the arbitration are expended on issues on which the successful party fails.[5] It might be argued that by this analogy the building owner who is permitted by an award under the Act to do work is the successful party, and should be entitled to his costs. It is submitted, however, that the analogy with normal arbitration is misleading. The right to carry out the work is conferred by the Act itself, which authorises certain things which would otherwise be an infringement of the property rights of the adjoining owner. The Act provides safeguards for the adjoining owner, most importantly by the provision of impartial resolution of the disputes under s 10. It would be inconsistent with the general scheme of the Act for the adjoining owner to be, in effect, obliged to pay for the very protection which the Act confers on him.

There may, however, be cases where the usual practice should be departed from. This could occur where for example the cost of the procedure was increased by unreasonable conduct by the adjoining owner or his surveyor, or where proposals were put forward on behalf of the adjoining owner that were completely unreasonable, but required the building owner's surveyor to carry out extensive work. A further point is that the liability is only for reasonable costs, and hence if the costs claimed are unreasonable in amount the building owner ought not to be required to pay them.

The categories of costs within s 10(13) include not only costs of making the award and of reasonable inspections, but also costs of 'any other matter arising out of the dispute' (s 10(13)(c)). The process of making the award may require the surveyors to determine difficult questions of law.[6] It is considered that it is within their discretion to take their own legal advice on such questions, and that the cost of such advice will be within s 10(13).

11.6   OTHER LIABILITIES OF BUILDING OWNER

In addition to his liabilities for expenses and costs, the building owner is under obligations to make payments under s 11(6) and (8), and to pay compensation under s 7. These matters have already been covered in Chapter 6.

---

5 *Lewis v Haverfordwest Rural District Council* [1953] 1 WLR 1486; *Demolition & Construction Co Ltd v Kent River Board* [1963] 2 Lloyd's Rep 7; *The Rozel* [1994] 2 Lloyd's Rep 161; *Metro-Cammell Hong Kong Ltd v FKI Engineering Plc* (1996) 77 BLR 84.

6 See eg para **15.4**.

11.7   RECOVERING EXPENSES FROM ADJOINING OWNER

Sections 13 and 14 contain provisions enabling the building owner to recover any expenses for which the adjoining owner is liable under s 11 by the following procedure.

11.7.1   Account

The building owner must serve an account on the adjoining owner under s 13(1). The requirements are as follows:

(a) It must be served within a 2-month period beginning on the day when the work, whose expenses the adjoining owner must (wholly or partially) pay, is completed. It might be thought that such a time-limit is merely directory, but in *Spiers and Son Ltd v Troup*,[7] time was held to be of the essence, so that a late account was ineffective.[8]

(b) It must be in writing, and must show:

   (i) particulars and expenses of the work;

   (ii) any deduction to which the adjoining owner or any other person is entitled in respect of old materials or otherwise.

(c) The work must be estimated and valued at fair average rates and prices according to the nature of the work, the locality, and the cost of labour and materials prevailing at the time when the work is executed.

11.7.2   Notice of objection

Within one month beginning with the date of service of the account the adjoining owner may serve a notice on the building owner stating any objection he has to the account. If he does so, a dispute is deemed to have arisen (s 13(2)), which must be resolved under s 10. If he does not, he is deemed to have no objection to the account (s 13(3)). This is the only area in which the Act imposes liability on the adjoining owner for failure to serve a notice. Whether time is of the essence of this time-limit does not appear ever to have been decided. It may be doubted whether the adjoining owner would be prevented from asserting an objection of substance out of time, although he might be condemned in costs.

---

7 (1915) 84 LJKB 1986.

8 That was a decision on s 96 of the 1894 Act, where the period was one month, but the language does not otherwise appear to be distinguishable.

11.8 SECTION 14

Once the account has been duly served, and any dispute about it resolved, the adjoining owner is liable to pay the sum due (s 14(1)). Further, by way of an unusual form of security, the property in the works to which the expenses (ie for which the adjoining owner is liable) relate vests solely in the building owner until the adjoining owner pays him (s 14(2)). For example, the adjoining owner may consent to a party wall under s 1(3), and it may be agreed or determined that he will pay half the expense, because he will make equal use of it. When the wall is built, half on the adjoining owner's land, it will nevertheless vest solely in the building owner until the adjoining owner pays his share, and until then it will be a trespass, which could be restrained by injunction, for the adjoining owner to make any use of his half of the wall. The following further points may be noted.

(a) Upon payment of the adjoining owner's contribution, the building owner's interest in the adjoining owner's half of the wall will presumably lapse, leaving the adjoining owner absolutely entitled to it, because it is on his side of the boundary, and part of his land. This is the force of the word 'until'. The building owner's interest is probably best regarded as a form of charge, securing the monetary liability, which is redeemed by payment.[9]

(b) Presumably, the building owner's interest will also lapse if he fails to serve any account under s 13, and thereby loses his right to enforce the adjoining owner's contribution.

(c) If the adjoining owner later makes greater use of the wall than was originally contemplated, he will become liable to an additional contribution under s 1(3)(b).[10] It is clear, however, that s 14(2) will not operate to vest any part of the wall in the building owner again, as security for this clawback, since the section applies only where an account has been served under s 13 (see s 14(1)).[11]

(d) It is considered that the interest conferred on the building owner is a property interest capable of binding successors in title of the adjoining owner.[12]

---

9 See *Mason v Fulham Corp* [1910] 1 KB 631.

10 The same will apply under s 11(11).

11 Dicta to the contrary in *Mason v Fulham Corp* [1910] 1 KB 631, where s 99 of the 1894 Act was considered, are no longer applicable since that section was not restricted in this way.

12 See further para **14.13.3**.

Chapter 12

SECURITY FOR EXPENSES

12.1 INTRODUCTION

Section 12 of the Act confers on both the building owner and the adjoining owner the right in certain circumstances to require the other to give security for expenses. The provisions derive from s 57 of the 1939 Act, save that under the 1939 Act disputes with regard to security were determined by the county court. Under the Act, disputes must be resolved in accordance with s 10.

Under s 12(1), the adjoining owner can serve a notice requiring the building owner, before he begins any work in exercise of the rights conferred by the Act, to give security to be agreed or determined in accordance with s 10. The rights of the building owner are provided for by s 12(2) and (3). He too must serve his notice before beginning work. He can require the adjoining owner to give security in two cases:

(a) where the adjoining owner requires the building owner to carry out any work the expenses of which are to be defrayed in whole or in part by the adjoining owner; and

(b) where the adjoining owner has served a notice requiring security.

In those cases, the building owner can serve a notice requiring the adjoining owner to give security as may be agreed or determined (s 12(2)). Subsection (3) provides that if within one month of the service of such a notice (by the building owner) or the dispute being determined under s 10, the adjoining owner does not comply with the notice or determination, his requirement (to the building owner to carry out work) or notice (to the building owner to give security) shall cease to have effect.

The aim of the section is to protect each party against default by the other in meeting the obligations imposed on him by various provisions of the Act. In the case of security being required from the building owner, the adjoining owner's interest is to ensure that the works the building owner is seeking to carry out will in fact be carried out and completed in a proper manner, and in accordance with any award made under s 10. Otherwise, the adjoining owner is at risk that the building owner might, for example, find himself financially unable to complete the works. The difficulties this can pose to the adjoining owner are self-evident: ultimately, without security for expenses he may be faced with no option but to carry out work himself at least to render the party wall safe and weatherproof, which in turn will involve him in invoking the procedures of the Act, and, presumably, subject to an award, bearing the expenses of the necessary work. Even if he successfully argues that the award should provide for the expenses of making good the party wall to be borne by the building owner whose original default has given rise to the problems,[1] this may be small practical comfort, because there will be no prospect of recovery from a building owner who has demonstrated inability to comply with the original award entitling him to carry out work.

In the case of security being given by the adjoining owner, considerations are different: the primary concern of the building owner will be to see that where he is to incur expense at the request of the adjoining owner, the adjoining owner will be able to reimburse him. The building owner is also entitled to apply for security simply because the adjoining owner has applied for security from him.

12.2   SECURITY BY THE BUILDING OWNER

The right of the adjoining owner must be exercised by a notice served before any work in exercise of the rights conferred by the Act is carried out (s 12(1)). Once such work starts, unless it is de minimis, the right to seek security in respect of it is lost. The notice must be served in accordance with s 15.[2] However, work which is not the subject matter of rights conferred by the Act carried out before the notice is served will not exclude the adjoining owner's rights. In the typical case of work to a party wall authorised by an award under s 10, therefore, work carried out on the building owner's building which is not subject to the provisions of the award will not count, even if it is part of a rebuilding scheme that will also involve the work to which the award relates.

The right to claim security is not expressly limited in any way. It is considered that it extends not only to the works which will be carried out, but to any claim to which their execution may give rise under the Act (including compensation under s 7(2) and allowance for disturbance under s 6(8)), or otherwise. But works not carried out under the Act, or claims arising from such works, would be beyond the scope of s 12. In the normal case of work authorised by an award, it will be necessary only to see what work the award covers in order to determine the extent of the matters in respect of which security can be required.

12.3   FACTORS

As to the matters to be taken into account, it is suggested that these must be grouped into two categories. First, those related to the work and, secondly, those related to the building owner.

---

1 For example under s 11(4)(b).
2 See generally Chapter 13.

12.3.1 Related to work

In the first category are all those costs and losses related to the work which may potentially have to be borne by the adjoining owner. They will include the following:

(a) costs which may fall on the adjoining owner if the building owner having commenced the work either proves unable to complete it, or carries it out defectively and does not remedy the defects;

(b) amounts to which the adjoining owner may be entitled under any award made under s 10, insofar as unpaid at the date of the adjoining owner's notice;

(c) amounts to which the adjoining owner may be contingently entitled under any award. For example, an award may make provision for compensation by the building owner of the adjoining owner in respect of damage caused by the works;

(d) amounts to which the adjoining owner may be entitled under s 1(7);

(e) amounts to which the adjoining owner may be entitled under s 11(8).

It is suggested, however, that the contingent entitlement of the adjoining owner under s 11(10), where the adjoining owner subsequently erects a building which is found to be more expensive by reason of special foundations on the adjoining owner's land, will not be taken into account in ordering security. The right of the adjoining owner will only arise once he has erected his building, established the increased costs, and delivered the necessary account and invoices. Accordingly, these future expenses are, it is suggested, too remote from the work to be taken into account.

Clearly, the weight to be given to the above factors and their financial consequences depend on the circumstances of the case. It will be necessary to take into account such matters as:

(a) the risk that the work may be more prolonged than foreseen;

(b) the risk that greater damage may occur than is currently envisaged;

(c) the existence or absence of a detailed method statement;

(d) the existence or absence of detailed structural calculations;

(e) the presence or absence of an appropriate design and supervisory team, having regard to the extent and risk of the works;

(f) the terms of any building contract including, in particular, preliminary items relating to temporary protection, shoring and precautions against damage.

12.3.2 Related to building owner

The second group of factors are those relating to the building owner. Primary among these will be financial standing. It would clearly be inappropriate in normal cases for a local authority, government department or substantial public company to be required to give security. On the other hand, a building owner who is bankrupt (or a company in liquidation) ought generally to be required to give security. The appointment of administrative receivers inevitably casts doubt on the future solvency of a company. The appointment of an administrator, or the existence of an individual voluntary arrangement or corporate voluntary arrangement would likewise be relevant factors. The residence of the building owner would also be relevant. If the building owner is not resident in England and Wales, there may be difficulty in enforcement of claims, and therefore security ought more readily to be considered.[3]

12.4 AMOUNT

The amount of security (if any) must be determined by balancing all relevant factors. The starting point may well be the realistic total of potential claims for which the building owner may be liable. This figure must, however, be discounted as appropriate, because the security, rather analogous to that afforded by a bond under a building contract, is to guard against the *risk* that the building owner will not fulfil his obligations. It is then necessary to consider the factors relating to the building owner himself. There will be a spectrum of situations, ranging from the well-funded building owner with a carefully planned programme of works involving little risk of damage to the adjoining owner's building, to cases where extensive and hazardous work is proposed on the basis of limited documentation by a building owner of doubtful financial worth. In the case of security under the Companies Act 1985 (s 726(1)), it is a general principle that security should not be oppressive, so as to stifle a genuine claim. It is submitted that whilst security should not be used indirectly as a way of placing unreasonable obstacles in the way of work which the Act entitles the building owner to carry out, it may not necessarily be unreasonable to order security in an amount which de facto prevents the particular building owner from proceeding.

12.5 PROCEDURE

Section 12(1) raises certain procedural difficulties and problems of interpretation that have not been addressed in the Act. First, the subsection does not make it clear what the consequences are of failure to give security.

---

3 This is, however, subject to the position of individual EU residents, see *Fitzgerald v Williams* [1996] 2 All ER 171, CA.

Does it, for example, prevent any start being made on the works? It is submitted that this must be the case, having regard to the wording of the subsection, and the fact that under subsections (2) and (3) an adjoining owner who fails to provide security loses his rights. Presumably, the adjoining owner and building owner are intended to be treated equally.

The Act does not prescribe any time-limit for the service of a notice requiring security. This omission can raise practical difficulties. If a notice under s 12 is delayed until after an award is made, a dispute about security will inevitably delay the work. This may in turn make it impossible to comply with the timetable, if any, laid down by the award, pursuant to s 10(12)(b). Presumably, the second award could then extend the time-limits in the first.

Section 12 nowhere in terms requires a dispute about security to be determined by the surveyors appointed to deal with other disputes. It is thought, however, that an attempt to refer the security dispute to different surveyors would be met by s 10(1) and (10). The words 'any matter connected with any work to which this Act relates' are wide enough to include security for the expenses of such works.

The fact remains that an adjoining owner has considerable scope for delaying the work by serving a notice requiring security at any time before the works actually start. No doubt, delay can legitimately influence the order for costs in the security award. In a bad case it might justify refusal of security.

12.6 MANNER OF GIVING SECURITY

In court proceedings, security is normally provided by way of payment into court. Under the 1939 Act this would have been the normal procedure, since questions as to security were dealt with by a county court judge. Under the Act, no guidance is given as to how security should be provided. The options appear to be:

(a) Depositing a sum in a bank account in the joint names of the surveyors. This has the advantage that the money is under the control of impartial experts who are familiar with the work and competent to assess the validity of any claim of recourse against the security. It is suggested that this will be by far the most convenient course.

(b) Security by bond, the condition of which is that if the building owner fulfils his obligations the bond shall become void, but otherwise remain in force. It may be necessary to consider whether the bond should be an 'on demand' bond or only one giving rise to liability on proof of loss. It is submitted that in general the latter will be appropriate.[4]

---

4 For the distinction see *Trafalgar House Construction (Regions) Ltd v General Surety Ltd & Guarantee Co Ltd* [1996] AC 199, HL.

(c) Parent company guarantee.

It is not clear under the Act what is to happen if the work in respect of which security is sought does not proceed. Presumably, in those circumstances, in general the security must be refunded, or, in the case of a bond or guarantee delivered up and cancelled. It is possible to envisage a situation where work is not begun within the statutory time-limit (ss 3(2)(b)(i) and 6(8)(a)) but the project is subsequently re-activated by a further notice. It is unclear whether in these circumstances the security provided in relation to the first notice must automatically be refunded, even though an identical request for security may be anticipated in relation to the second notice. Principle would suggest that this is indeed the case, but refunding might be stopped by a further application for security before it has taken place.

12.7 SECURITY BY ADJOINING OWNER

The building owner's right to ask for security arises in two cases. The first is where the adjoining owner requires the building owner to carry out any work the expenses of which are to be defrayed in whole or in part by the adjoining owner (s 12(2)(a)). Only expenses within s 11(7) and (9) result from a requirement of the adjoining owner. The scope of the security which can be ordered is therefore limited to these expenses. Subject to this, the power to order security is subject to the same considerations as already discussed.

The second case in which an adjoining owner may be ordered to give security is more general, and arises simply where the adjoining owner has served a notice requiring the building owner to give security (s 12(2)(b)). The principle behind granting such a tit-for-tat right to the building owner is unclear and sits uncomfortably with the general principle of s 11(1) that expenses are to be borne by the building owner. Nevertheless, there are several cases in which the Act requires the adjoining owner to contribute to the expense of works,[5] and some of these cases are not covered by s 12(2)(a). Security for these expenses can evidently be ordered under this section, and the same considerations regarding the amount and manner of security will apply as already discussed. If the proposed work does not include any operation whose expenses will have to be borne, or shared, by the adjoining owner, there cannot be any ground for ordering him to give security.

---

5 See para **11.4**.

Chapter 13

SERVICE OF NOTICES

13.1 INTRODUCTION

The Act requires notices to be served in many contexts. These are covered in the chapters on the individual topics dealt with by the Act. A check-list of the notices for which the Act provides is contained in Appendix 3. This chapter considers the formal requirements of the notices required by the Act, the methods of service, and the effect of non-service.

13.2 FORMAL REQUIREMENTS OF NOTICES

Although the Act does not specifically say so, it is clear that all notices required to be given under its provisions must be in writing since they invariably have to be 'served'. The Act, like the 1939 Act, does not prescribe any particular form of notice. Therefore, any notice which contains the particulars required by the relevant provision of the Act will be sufficient.[1]

Whether a document constitutes a proper notice under the provisions of the Act falls to be decided, therefore, on general principles. In order to satisfy the relevant provisions of the Act the notice must be in terms that are sufficiently clear and intelligible to bring home to the ordinary recipient the fact that the building owner or adjoining owner, as the case may be, is purporting to exercise a right under the Act, and to enable him to see what counter-notice he should give or what other action he should take.[2] Having regard to the strictness with which courts have approached interpretation of the 1939 Act,[3] it is suggested that the notice must specify with reasonable precision what action the giver of the notice proposes to take, and the provision of the Act which authorises him to take it. For example, a notice under s 3 should, it is submitted, specify within which paragraphs of s 2(2) the work proposed by the building owner falls. The details of the work should be such as to enable a fair idea to be gathered of the extent and nature of the proposals, but it will be unnecessary to include a full analysis of the work, for example by way of a bill of quantities, structural calculations, and drawings relating to details. The information must be sufficient to enable the recipient of the notice both to know what is proposed, and to decide what action is necessary in order to protect his interests, and (where necessary) to instruct a surveyor.

---

1 For forms of notice see Appendix 4.
2 Compare *Hobbs Hart & Co v Grover* [1899] 1 Ch 11 (a decision on s 91 of the London Building Act 1894); *Nunes v Davies Laing & Dick Ltd* [1986] 1 EGLR 106.
3 As in *Gyle-Thompson v Wall Street (Properties) Ltd* [1974] 1 All ER 295.

13.3   AMENDMENT OF NOTICE

The Act makes no provision for amendment of notices. It is submitted that no amendment is possible, unless both parties concur in treating the amendment as included in the original notice. But the surveyors ought to give notices a reasonably liberal construction, so as to avoid delay and expense arising from the need to serve fresh notices.

13.4   MODE OF SERVICE

Section 15 of the Act provides for service. Section 15(1) provides three primary methods of service. Section 15(2) provides two alternative methods where the Act requires or authorises a notice or other document to be served on a person as owner of premises. These alternatives will not apply to all the notices required by the Act, since some have to be served on occupiers (eg under s 8). These prescribed methods are not compulsory or exhaustive, and do not preclude proof of service by other means.

The three primary methods of service authorised by s 15(1) are:

(a)   delivery to the recipient in person.

(b)   service by post to the recipient's usual or last known residence or place of business in the UK;

(c)   in the case of a body corporate, delivery to the secretary or clerk of the body corporate at its registered or principal office or service by post to the secretary or clerk of that body corporate at that office.

13.4.1   Personal delivery

By analogy with the rules governing personal service of writs, it is suggested that:

(a)   handing the notice to an agent of the recipient will not be sufficient, unless this is at the request of the recipient.[4]

(b)   the document must be left with and not merely shown to the recipient.

13.4.2   Postal service on an individual

Service by post requires that the letter containing the notice be properly addressed, pre-paid and posted to the proper address of the person to be served. If the letter is returned through the post office as undelivered, it will not be treated as having been served.[5] By s 7 of the Interpretation Act 1978, it is provided that where an Act authorises or requires any document to be served by

---

4 *Montgomery, Jones & Co v Liebenthal & Co* [1898] 1 QB 487.
5 *R v London County Quarter Sessions Appeals Committee ex parte Rossi* [1956] 1 All ER 670.

post, service is deemed to be effective by properly addressing, pre-paying, and posting a letter containing the document and, unless the contrary is proved, to have been effected at the time at which the letter would be delivered in the ordinary course of post. It has been held that where a notice has to be served by a certain time, it is open to a party on whom it is served by post to prove either that he in fact received it later than ordinary course of post, or that he did not receive the document at all.[6]

13.4.3   Postal address

The address to which the letter is posted must be to the 'usual or last-known residence or place of business in the United Kingdom'. The United Kingdom includes England, Wales, Scotland and Northern Ireland, but not the Republic of Ireland, or the Channel Islands. 'Sending' a document by post involves the whole process of transmission from server to recipient, so that if a letter is incorrectly addressed, but subsequently re-directed by the post office to the correct address it will be validly served by post.[7] 'Last known' has been held to mean 'last known to the giver of the notice'.[8] In *National Westminster Bank Ltd v Betchworth Investments Ltd*,[9] it was said that 'last known address' were words in ordinary usage in English. The test is what would the ordinary person regard as the last known address of the person in question. In that case, the last known address of a company was said to be its registered office, not its managing agent's office.

13.4.4   Service on a body corporate

Section 15(1)(c) provides two alternative methods of service, which apply not only to limited companies but also to other bodies corporate such as local authorities. In regard to limited companies, s 725 of the Companies Act 1985 provides for service of documents by leaving the document at the registered office of the company, or sending it to the registered office by post. The document can be validly served by recorded delivery.[10]

13.5   OTHER METHODS OF SERVICE

The reference in s 15(1)(b) to 'post' includes registered post and recorded delivery as well as the ordinary post. Further, it is possible for irregularities of

---

6   *R v London Quarter Sessions Appeal Committee ex parte Rossi* [1956] 1 All ER 670; *Maltglade Ltd v St Albans Rural District Council* [1972] 3 All ER 129.

7   *Austin Rover Group Ltd v Crouch Butler Savage Associates (A Firm) and Others* [1986] 3 All ER 50, CA.

8   Ibid.

9   [1975] 1 EGLR 57, CA.

10   *TO Supplies (London) Ltd v Jerry Creighton Ltd* [1951] 2 All ER 992. Recorded Delivery Service Act 1962, s 1.

service to be waived by the recipient of the notice taking action on it. It is also possible for the parties to agree an alternative method of service of notices, for example by agreeing that notices shall be exchanged between their respective surveyors.

13.6   SERVICE ON THE OWNER OF PREMISES

Section 15(2) makes additional provision where a notice or other document is authorised or required to be served on a person as owner of premises. It provides for the notice to be addressed to 'the owner' (ie without naming him) of the premises (which must be named), and for delivery of it to a person on the premises, or if no person to whom it can be delivered is found there, fixing it to a conspicuous part of the premises.[11] This provision appears to apply to almost all the notices required by the Act, since building and adjoining owners are required to be served as owners of their respective premises. But it does not apply where service is required on an occupier (eg under s 8(3)).

13.7   PERSONS ON WHOM NOTICES MUST BE SERVED

The Act clearly contemplates the need to serve multiple notices. In work to which the Act relates, there may be numerous persons who satisfy the description of adjoining owner. All of them must be served with notices, even if the work proposed will not affect them directly. There can also be more than one building owner, but the adjoining owner's task is simplified: he need only respond to the notice served on him, and need not (and indeed has no right to) seek to serve any counter-notice on other persons who might satisfy the definition of building owner. However, it is open to the recipient of a notice to question the validity of it on the basis that it has not been served by all those persons by whom it should have been served, as for example where two persons together constituted the 'building owner', but the notice was served by only one of them.[12]

13.8   JOINT OWNERS

Where there are joint building owners, notices must be served by or on behalf of all of them.[13] But where there are joint adjoining owners, it has been held sufficient to serve only one.[14]

---

11 Compare Law of Property Act 1925, s 196(3).
12 *Lehmann v Herman* [1993] 1 EGLR 172.
13 Ibid.
14 *Crosby v Alhambra Co Ltd* [1907] 1 Ch 295.

13.9 FAILURE TO SERVE NOTICES

It is an essential precondition of a building owner's exercise of rights under the Act that he has served the relevant notices under ss 1, 3 or 6. Failure to do this cannot be cured by any subsequent 'award' purporting to authorise the work to be done, which will itself be a nullity.[15] Failure by an adjoining owner to serve a counter-notice consenting to works proposed by the building owner will not in general prejudice the adjoining owner's position, and indeed in the case of s 1(3) of the Act he would seem positively ill-advised to serve such a notice because of the onerous responsibilities which will then be placed on him. In general, the adjoining owner if in doubt is probably best advised simply not to respond to a notice served by the building owner, provided he wishes to protect his position and instruct a surveyor. Since the building owner is normally obliged to pay for the works and the surveyor's costs and expenses, the adjoining owner usually has little incentive to serve a notice consenting to the works. But if he is content to accept the building owner's party structure notice subject only to the modifications contemplated by s 4, the service of a counter-notice can reduce the area of dispute, and so save costs. Only s 13(2) (notice of objection to an account) imposes liability on an adjoining owner for failure to serve notice.

13.10 WAIVER OF TIME-LIMITS OR IRREGULARITIES IN NOTICES

The timetable laid down by the Act is, it is submitted, capable of being enlarged by agreement between the parties or their surveyors with their authority. The time-limits are inserted for the protection of the recipient of the notice, and are therefore capable of being waived. There is no public interest involved which would require the court to adopt a stricter approach.[16] The same principle would apply to other irregularities in notices. The policy of the Act is to facilitate dispute resolution. If the parties accept that irregular notices are to be treated as valid, the surveyors would, it is suggested, be entitled to proceed on this basis, since the parties would be estopped by convention from denying that the relevant notices were valid.[17]

---

15 *Gyle-Thompson v Wall Street (Properties) Ltd* [1971] 1 All ER 295; *Lehmann v Herman* [1993] 1 EGLR 172.
16 Compare *Kammin's Ballrooms Co Ltd v Zenith Investments (Torquay) Ltd* [1970] 2 All ER 871 – statutory time-limit capable of being waived.
17 *Amalgamated Investment and Property Co Ltd v Texas Commerce International Bank Ltd* [1981] 3 All ER 577.

Chapter 14

SUCCESSORS IN TITLE

14.1 INTRODUCTION

The Act is concerned with owners of pieces of adjoining land. It gives them rights, and imposes on them liabilities, some of which are contingent on the occurrence of events at an indefinite time in the future. Yet the Act contains no general provision explaining how successors in title are affected, if at all. So long as the adjoining lands remain in the same hands as when the initiating notice is served, the effect of the Act is relatively clear. But as soon as one or both of the adjoining parcels of land change hands, difficult questions arise which the Act does not expressly answer. This can happen before or after the award.

14.2 DEFINITIONS

Granted that the Act deals fully with the rights and liabilities of the original building owner and adjoining owner, the questions which arise, however, concern the rights and liabilities of their successors in title. The material available for answering the questions consists of (a) the Act itself; and (b) the general principles of property law. So far as the Act is concerned, the starting point is the definitions of 'building owner' and 'adjoining owner'. These have already been outlined (see para **2.5**). They give rise to a number of points.

(a) 'Building owner' means an owner of land 'who is desirous of exercising rights under the Act'. Thus he is defined not by the land which he owns, but by his desire, a personal attribute, which will not necessarily be shared by his successor in title.

(b) 'Adjoining owner' means an owner of land adjoining that of the building owner. This is a definition which assumes the existence of a neighbouring building owner, and therefore depends not only on the land owned, but also on the personal attribute of the neighbour.

(c) The personal nature of these definitions can be illustrated by reference to the building owner who ceases to desire to build (eg because he has completed his operations). He thereupon ceases to be a building owner. And because there is no longer a building owner, there is no longer an adjoining owner. The definitions do not run with the land.

(d) It follows that whenever the Act gives rights to, or imposes liabilities on, the building owner or the adjoining owner as such, it is at least arguable, as a matter of language, that those rights and liabilities accrue only to the persons (if any) answering the definitions at the material time, and not to any successors of theirs. This is what the Act does, except in a single context (s 11(10)).

(e) On the other hand, it must be kept in mind that the definitions in s 20 apply 'unless the context otherwise requires'. If the 'personal' construction suggested above produces a result which is wholly unreasonable or capricious, it may therefore be permissible to adopt another, reasonable, construction.

(f) In particular contexts, these approaches can give rise to acute conflict. For example, under s 11(10) a contribution may become payable to the adjoining owner long after the original building owner has ceased to satisfy the definition. The personal construction suggests that only the original adjoining owner can benefit, since his successors are not within the definition. But the policy behind the section suggests that such a narrow construction would defeat its object.[1]

14.3   ASSIGNABILITY: BENEFIT AND BURDEN

Property law suggests a supplementary approach. The rights and liabilities created by the Act may be considered in terms of their assignability.

(a) Rights and liabilities may be real (ie annexed to land) or personal. As has been shown, the nature of the definitions of building owner and adjoining owner means that rights and liabilities conferred and imposed on them by those descriptions are likely to be personal. There is only one context in which the Act confers a right by reference to a land-based description (s 11(10)). And apart from the rights of entry under s 8, there is only one context where the Act clearly imposes a liability which is annexed to land (s 14(2)).

(b) Real rights and liabilities run with the land to which they are annexed, affecting its successive owners according to the principles of real property law.

(c) Personal rights do not normally run with the land automatically but are usually assignable expressly. Rights created by statute can usually be assigned either at law[2] or in equity. A few rights are not assignable at all.[3]

(d) Personal liabilities, however, are in general not assignable.

---

1 See para **5.7.2**(b).
2 Under the Law of Property Act 1925, s 136.
3 For example a bare cause of action: see *Trendtex Trading Corp v Credit Suisse* [1982] AC 679.

14.4   BEFORE AWARD: DISPUTE PROCEDURE

We can now turn to the specific problems posed by changes of ownership at particular times. The first time span is the period during which the machinery of the Act is being operated, ie from the service of the initiating notice by the building owner until the date of the resulting award.

14.5   AGREEMENT

It is always open to the parties to reach agreement outside the Act's procedures. If this happens the effect on successors must depend on the application of ordinary common law principles (see above) to the contract. In general, benefits will be assignable, but not burdens, and so on. If the agreement is by deed, it may also grant rights in land (eg easements) which will bind successors. If the agreement arises from the service of a notice of consent under the Act, it is considered that a binding contract arises for the works to be carried out in the manner provided by the Act: the benefit will be assignable to a new building owner, and the adjoining owner's successor (who will satisfy the definition of adjoining owner until the work is complete) will be bound by the statutory rights of entry.[4]

14.6   DISPUTE

If the parties cannot agree, a dispute ensues and surveyors are appointed. What if one party sells his land before they have made an award? What is the new owner's standing in the dispute? Is he entitled to step into his predecessor's shoes? Can he insist on the procedure starting again from the beginning? There are no authoritative answers to these questions. The extreme view is that the personal nature of the rights under the Act means that any succession technically requires the procedure to be started again, and that any new party can insist on this. This view is inconvenient, and open to abuse (eg by an adjoining owner who wishes at all costs to delay the start of works). It is also, it is submitted, incorrect. The personal nature of the Act's definitions does not affect the procedure leading to an award, because until then there is always a building owner desiring to build, and therefore an adjoining owner, within the definitions. This suggests further consequences.

(a)   Since they satisfy the definitions, it is submitted that it is open to the new owners to step in and adopt the proceedings taken by their predecessors, at any rate provided they are prepared to accept the burdens (eg payment of expenses and costs) as well as the benefits.

---

4 Consent under s 1(3) leaves further matters undecided, which may still lead to a dispute.

(b) Even if that is wrong, the rights created by notices served under the Act are, it is submitted, capable of assignment, so that the new owner can be put in a position to adopt the proceedings by express assignment. The right to have a dispute determined in accordance with all the provisions of the Act is a benefit to both parties, and although the burdens may not be technically assignable, the assignment will be subject to the accrued rights of the other party,[5] as will adoption of the proceedings. The assignment is not of a bare cause of action, since it affects the assignee's land.

14.7   DISSENTING SUCCESSOR

The question remains whether a successor who does not wish to adopt the proceedings can be bound by them.

14.7.1   Building owner

This question is unlikely to affect a building owner, because the remedy is in his own hand. He can insist that his vendor withdraws his notice, or otherwise determines the existing proceedings, and then serve his own notice.

14.7.2   Adjoining owner

The question arises acutely in the case of a dissenting adjoining owner. If he refuses to take part in the existing proceedings, can they lead to an award binding on him? Or is the building owner bound to start afresh by serving a new notice on him? Policy considerations pull both ways. On the one hand, it may seem unjust for an adjoining owner to be bound by deliberations between surveyors he has not chosen, and who have not heard him. On the other, the building owner may be severely prejudiced by the delay, especially if an unscrupulous adjoining owner is able to keep moving his land from one person to another. It is submitted that, provided the new owner purchased with notice of the dispute, this is a mere procedural question, which ought to be dealt with by analogy with proceedings in court. The new adjoining owner satisfies the definition in the Act, and is therefore a proper party to the dispute. The transfer of the land to him does not affect the building owner's claim: it is no more than a devolution of the original adjoining owner's interest. In litigation, it would be a matter of course for the new owner to be substituted as a party.[6] Subject to directions protecting his interest as far as necessary (eg notification of all that has happened in the dispute; opportunity to make representations; decision to be made by third surveyor, if he wishes), there seems to be no reason why the new owner should not be substituted as a party to the dispute under the Act. On that footing no new notice need be served, and the award will bind him

5 See Snell, *Principles of Equity* 29th edn (Sweet & Maxwell, 1991) p 81.
6 See Rules of the Supreme Court 1965, Ord 15, r 7; County Court Rules 1981, Ord 5, r 11.

whether he participates in the procedure or not. This, however, may not apply to a purchaser who has purchased without any notice of the dispute.[7]

14.8 AFTER AWARD

An award gives rise to a series of rights and liabilities which are immediate, in the sense that they are immediately defined (although monetary liabilities will not be payable until they are quantified, which will not be until the works are completed). There are other rights and liabilities which may subsequently arise under the Act, but which are contingent on the occurrence of defined circumstances in the future. It is convenient to distinguish between these categories of immediate and contingent rights and liabilities.

14.9 IMMEDIATE RIGHTS AND LIABILITIES

The principal immediate rights and liabilities are the right of the building owner to carry out works defined by the award, and the liability of the adjoining owner (under s 8) to allow entry for the purpose. Since the works will take a certain amount of time, and more time will pass before the consequential financial liabilities are quantified, there is plenty of leeway for either party's land to change hands before the rights are exhausted and the liabilities discharged. Which rights and liabilities will devolve on the successors?

14.9.1 Rights (benefit)

Just as contractual benefits are, in general, assignable, so it is considered that the rights conferred by an award are assignable, so that a building owner can assign to his successor his rights of entry, and his rights to any payments due from the adjoining owner on completion of the works. Indeed, *Mason v Fulham Corp*[8] suggests that rights will pass automatically with a conveyance of the building owner's land, unless expressly reserved. But *Re Stone and Hastie*[9] suggests there is no such assignment on the grant of a lease.

14.9.2 Liabilities (burden)

Contractual burdens cannot be assigned. Nor can a building owner's immediate liability under an award: it is personal to him, and he cannot escape it by conveying to a man of straw.[10] It is considered that the same applies to the

---

7 See para **14.13.1**.
8 [1910] 1 KB 631. This case actually concerns an agreement, not an award, and a contingent, not immediate, right.
9 [1903] 2 KB 463. This case concerns an award, but again, a contingent right.
10 See *Selby v Whitbread & Co* [1917] 1 KB 736.

immediate financial liabilities of the adjoining owner. But his successor will be bound by the liabilities which affect the land itself (ie the rights of entry under s 8, and the vesting of the works under s 14(2)).

14.10   CONTINGENT RIGHTS AND LIABILITIES

There are three sections under which contingent financial liabilities may arise at some indefinite time in the future. They are as follows:

(a) Section 1(3)(b), which provides for the allocation of expenses where the adjoining owner has consented. 'The two owners' are to bear them 'from time to time' in a proportion which pays regard to the use they make of the wall. Thus, either owner may at any time or times become liable for an additional contribution whether or not he paid anything in the first instance.

(b) Section 11(11) deals with similar subject matter. It applies where an adjoining owner makes use of work originally paid for entirely by the building owner. It imposes liability only on the adjoining owner, and only where he made no contribution in the first instance.

(c) Section 11(10) is concerned with special foundations, and requires 'the owner of the building to which the foundations belong' to make a contribution to later building expenses of the adjoining owner, if they impede him. This provision has been considered above (para **5.7.2**).

It cannot be every increase in use, however trivial, which will trigger liability for clawbacks under ss 1(3)(b) and 11(11). No doubt, there will need to be works requiring a notice under the Act to be served. The award will then take into account the allocation of expenses on the earlier occasion.[11] There is no uniformity of benefit and burden between the cases. Under s 1(3)(b), either party may serve the notice, and the contingent liability will fall upon him; under s 11(11) only the former adjoining owner will serve the notice and incur the liability; under s 11(10), again the notice will be by the former adjoining owner, but the liability will fall on his neighbour.

14.10.1   Rights (benefit)

There are two leading cases concerned with the devolution of the contingent right to a clawback payment (under the equivalent of s 11(11)).

In *Re Stone and Hastie* (above) the original building owner had leased his property on a 21-year term, and an award upon a later notice by the adjoining owner directed payment of a clawback to the lessee. It was held that the lessee was not entitled to it, and the award was to that extent void.

---

11 As happened in *Re Stone and Hastie* (above).

On the other hand, in *Mason v Fulham Corp* (above), the original building owner sold his property and a clawback payment was later made to the purchaser. The original building owner thereupon claimed that the payment should have been made to him, but it was held that the right had passed (without mention) to his successor in title. If the reasoning is less than satisfactory (since it ignored the difficulties that the purchaser did not satisfy the definition of building owner, and the right was not annexed to the land), the result is realistic.

The principle to be deduced from these decisions is that, in the absence of express reservation[12] or assignment, the benefit of a contingent right will pass with the freehold, but not with a derivative interest. It is thought unlikely that this principle will be disturbed. It will presumably apply also to clawbacks under s 1(3)(b). The special difficulties posed by the wording of s 11(10) are considered elsewhere (paras **5.7.2**(b) and **14.2**(f)): if (as is suggested there) the benefit is capable of passing, this principle will presumably apply to it.

14.10.2 Liabilities (burden)

Under s 11(10), the wording is deliberately designed to make the burden of the contingent liability fall on successors of the building owner. But there is a serious question as to whether the contingent liability for clawbacks under ss 1(3)(b) and 11(11) is capable of binding successors.[13] One further argument may be noticed here. It is established that the benefit of the clawback under s 11(11) can pass,[14] so that the reference to the building owner in that section is treated as including successors.[15] It would be surprising, therefore, if the reference to the adjoining owner in the same section should not be treated in the same way, and s 1(3)(b) is a shortened provision which must take its colour from s 11(11). No authority has been found in which this question has been considered.[16] On the assumption that the contingent liabilities are not restricted to the original parties, the following features may be noted.

(a) They will fall upon the relevant owner at some future date. There is no provision of the Act which charges them on the land,[17] but they are incidents which affect the owner because of his ownership.

---

12 See *Mason v Fulham Corporation* (above), at p 639.

13 See para **14.2**.

14 See *Mason v Fulham Corporation* (above).

15 See the headnote in the *Mason* case, which expresses the sense, rather than the words, of the judgments.

16 In *Re Stone and Hastie* (above), the adjoining owner against whom a clawback was awarded was holding under a long lease which appears to have been granted by the original adjoining owner (see p 468): but there was no appeal on the ground that the liability had not passed to him, and no discussion of this issue.

17 Section 14(2) applies only to immediate liabilities: see para **11.8**(b).

(b) Normally, they will arise when the owner wishes to build, and serves a notice under the Act. At that stage they become immediate liabilities of the new building owner, to be determined by the award, and no doubt they are personal to him like his other immediate liabilities.[18]

14.11 CONVEYANCING IMPLICATIONS

The standard works on conveyancing[19] contain no material reference to the party walls legislation. No doubt this is partly because of its local application. But it is clear from the Act's effect on successors in title that conveyancers will have to pay more attention to it, now that its application is countrywide.

14.12 LIABILITIES AFFECTING A PURCHASER

The foregoing survey has considered what liabilities arising under the Act will bind a purchaser. They can be categorised as follows.

14.12.1 Purchaser from building owner

If a building owner sells, whether before or after award, the purchaser from him is in relatively little jeopardy. He will in principle be liable for works which he undertakes, but not for those already undertaken by his vendor. Contingent liabilities affecting him can arise only in the unusual cases of s 1(3)(b) (where the original notice was consented to) and s 11(10) (where the works included special foundations).

14.12.2 Purchaser from adjoining owner

The exposure of a purchaser from an adjoining owner is considerably greater. If the sale is before award, he is buying a dispute to which he may become an unwilling party. If the sale is after award, he may be bound by:

(a) the building owner's rights of entry;

(b) the vesting of works in the building owner (s 14(2));

(c) the contingent clawback provisions (ss 1(3)(b) and 11(11)).

---

18 See para **14.9.2**.
19 *Emmett on Title* (FT Law & Tax) and Ruoff and Roper, *Registered Conveyancing* 6th edn (Sweet & Maxwell).

14.13   REGISTRATION AS LAND CHARGE

Are any of these liabilities registrable as land charges, so as to be discoverable by normal conveyancing processes?

14.13.1   Dispute

The dispute arising from the service of a notice, although analogous to a pending land action, is not within the statutory definition because it is not 'pending in court'.[20] It therefore appears that a purchaser who purchases without notice of the dispute may be entitled to insist that the procedure be started afresh by service of a new notice on him. On the other hand, if an award is appealed into the county court, the proceedings thereupon satisfy the definition and should be registered immediately, or a purchaser without express notice will not be bound by them.[21]

14.13.2   Rights of entry

Rights of entry under s 8 are not legal interests in the normal sense,[22] and it is considered that they are probably not registrable as equitable easements (although the contrary is arguable) in view of the restricted construction given to that term.[23] Be that as it may, there appears to be no incentive to register them, since non-registration will not enable a purchaser to escape them. They are not like rights originating in private grant which, if registrable, will be lost once and for all by non-registration. Even if a purchaser can technically take free of the rights of entry triggered by a notice served on his vendor, the most the building owner need do is serve a fresh 14-day notice on him. The right of entry is then exercisable against the land by force of s 8.

14.13.3   Vesting of works

If the adjoining owner has not paid his immediate liabilities under an award, the works on his side of the boundary will still be vested in the building owner under s 14(2). It is considered that this gives the building owner (without any application by him) a charge for expenses incurred by him under the Act, which is therefore within the definition of a Class B land charge.[24] The building owner should therefore register such a charge as soon as he serves his account, or it will be void against the purchaser.[25]

---

20 See Land Charges Act 1972, s 17(1).

21 Ibid, s 5(7).

22 Since they do not fall within the Law of Property Act 1925, s 1(2)(e). But rights under the Act are not mere equitable rights: see *Selby v Whitbread & Co* [1917] 1 KB 736, 747.

23 See *Ives (ER) Investment Ltd v High* [1967] 2 QB 379; *Poster v Slough Estates Ltd* [1969] 1 Ch 495; *Shiloh Spinners Ltd v Harding* [1973] AC 691.

24 See Land Charges Act 1972, s 2(2), (3).

25 If the land is registered, he can protect the charge by notice under s 49(1)(c) of the Land Registration Act 1925, or the procedure under ibid s 59(2) proviso, and Land Registration Rules 1925, r 155.

14.13.4   Contingent liabilities

The contingent liabilities are mere personal liabilities which attach to the owner (if at all: see para **14.10.2**) because of his ownership of the land at the material time. They are not charged on the land, and are therefore not registrable, although their potential existence will be deducible from the award.

14.14   ACTION FOR CONVEYANCERS

It is evident that the Act may give rise to liabilities affecting a purchaser which fall outside the modern systems of registration. It is beyond the scope of this book to attempt a detailed analysis of the consequences for conveyancers. The following steps are suggested.

14.14.1   Before contract

The purchaser will wish to know whether there is about to be, or ever has been, an award which will affect him. Preliminary enquiries should be directed to the following issues:

(a) Whether there is currently a dispute on foot, and if so:
   - what notices have been served (including consent notices);
   - what appointments of surveyors have been made;
   - what stage the surveyors have reached in their deliberations.

(b) Whether any award has been made at any time which affects the property, and if so:
   - is it an old award, in the sense that all the works have been carried out, and immediate liabilities discharged; or
   - is it a new award, in the sense that the works have not yet been completed.

(c) If there is an old award:
   - did the work include special foundations;
   - were the expenses borne solely by the building owner.[26]

(d) If there is a new award:
   - are there any expenses to be borne by the adjoining owner;
   - has any account been served for them.

(e) Whether any works have ever been carried out under the Act by consent, and if so:
   - what notices were served (including any counter-notice);
   - were any expenses borne by the adjoining owner.

---

26 These enquiries go to contingent liabilities under s 11(10), (11).

14.14.2 Contract

(a) If there is a dispute in progress, or work still proceeding under a new award:
- the parties will have to consider how immediate liabilities are to be shared between them, and to agree upon appropriate indemnities;
- the purchaser should consider insisting on the express assignment of the benefit of all notices served, or of the award.

(b) If there is an old award:
- the vendor should sell subject to the award;
- the purchaser should seek to acquire the benefit of the award expressly.[27]

14.14.3 Completion

(a) Subject to contrary agreement, the property should be conveyed subject to and with the benefit of: (i) any current notices under the Act; and (ii) any award.

(b) If the land is registered, it will be more appropriate to embody this transaction in a separate document.

14.14.4 Land charges

The following matters appear to be registrable under the Land Charges Act 1972[28] (although it is not the current practice of conveyancers to register them).

(a) An appeal against an award will be registrable as a pending land action.

(b) The vesting of works in the building owner appears to be a Class B land charge.

(c) It is perhaps arguable that the rights of entry arising from an award are registrable as equitable easements (Class D(iii)).

14.14.5 Registered land

If the land is registered, the land charges under (a) and (b) above should be protected by notice under s 49(1)(c) of the Land Registration Act 1925. Equitable easements, however, are overriding interests,[29] which need no mention on the register.

---

27 These provisions go to the contingent rights and liabilities.
28 See para **14.13**.
29 Land Registration Act 1925, s 70(1)(a).

14.15   SHORTCOMINGS

It is regrettable that the Act has not taken the opportunity to clear up the ancient ambiguity about the standing of successors in title. What is more disturbing is the failure to adapt the machinery of the Act to the registration regimes of modern conveyancing. Registration ensures, so far as reasonably possible, that purchasers of land do not find themselves saddled with liabilities that they could not have discovered. Detailed enquiries are all very well, but not an adequate substitute. It may be that a purchaser from an adjoining owner is sure to learn of a current dispute under the Act, and can only be kept in ignorance of it by misrepresentation. But the same is not true of an award which is some years old. Unregistered documents fall out of sight quickly, and a vendor who knows nothing of an award made before his time will without fault give unhelpful answers to enquiries. But the purchaser's ignorance will not, of itself, protect him from contingent liabilities which may arise from the provisions of a forgotten award.

Chapter 15

RELATIONSHIP WITH OTHER AREAS OF LAW

15.1 INTRODUCTION

The rights conferred by the Act impinge on various other areas of the law relating to the relationship between building and adjoining owners. In general, it may be said that the provisions of the Act are not intended to affect other rights except to the extent necessary in order to give effect to the purposes of the Act. On second reading the Earl of Lytton said:

> 'The Bill will have no effect on title. The wall owned by one party or another is not a party wall, nor does it cut across provisions for easements contained in titles. It is not designed to affect common law rights of support or conflict with other statutory requirements ... the Bill dovetails in with the Access to Neighbouring Land Act. I am satisfied that there is no conflict with that. Statutory consents such as planning, listed buildings and Building Regulations will be unaffected ...'[1]

In general, this intention is achieved by s 9(a), but there are nevertheless a number of important subsidiary points that require clarification.

15.2 COMMON LAW RIGHTS IN PARTY WALLS

At common law, the expression 'party wall' had no precise meaning. It included four categories of wall:

(a) a wall owned by both owners as tenants in common;

(b) a wall divided into longitudinal halves, one half being owned by each owner;

(c) a wall belonging entirely to one owner, subject to an easement in favour of the other owner, to have it maintained as a dividing wall;

(d) a wall longitudinally divided, each half being subject to an easement of support in favour of the other half.[2]

The Law of Property Act 1925, abolished legal tenancies in common, and contained provisions which had the effect of subjecting walls in category (a) to a trust for sale, and moving them into category (d).[3] Thus, at common law the extent to which either owner could carry out work affecting the whole of a party wall without either trespassing upon the other's property, or interfering with his easement, was severely restricted.

---

1 Hansard HL Debates, Vol 568, 31 Jan 1996, Cols 1536, 1540.
2 See *Watson v Gray* (1880) 14 Ch D 192.
3 See s 38 and first Sch, Pt V para 1.

15.3   SECTION 9

The machinery of the Act enables the building owner to carry out work affecting the whole of a party wall, notwithstanding the adjoining owner's rights at common law. But s 9 provides that:

> 'Nothing in this Act shall—
>
> (a)   authorise any interference with an easement of light or other easements in or relating to a party wall; or
>
> (b)   prejudicially affect any right of any person to preserve or restore any right or other thing in or connected with a party wall in case of the party wall being pulled down or rebuilt.'

15.3.1   Section 9(a)

This subsection expressly protects an adjoining owner's rights of light, and also his other easements relating to the party wall, of which the most obvious is the easement of support. These rights are considered separately below. What may be noted here is that this provision does not prohibit temporary interference with such rights during the carrying out of works. The works which the Act authorises to be carried out necessarily involve physical interference with the party wall, removal of support, and often interference with the access of light. The common law rights of the adjoining owner to prevent these invasions are necessarily overridden temporarily, so that the authorised work can be carried out. What this subsection ensures is that the invasion is only temporary, and that the adjoining owner's established easements must continue once the works are complete.

15.3.2   Section 9(b)

It is difficult to attach any sensible meaning to the words 'prejudicially affect any right ... to preserve or restore any *right* or other thing in or connected with a party wall'. A right is not a thing: nor is it clear what right there can be to preserve or restore any right in a party wall. The phrase has an intriguing statutory history, which partly illuminates the mystery.

(a)   In s 101 of the 1894 Act the wording was 'take away abridge or prejudicially affect any right of any person to preserve or restore any *light* or other thing ...'. In this context, it is clear that 'light' means an aperture to receive light (as in the expression 'leaded lights'), ie a thing.

(b)   Section 127 of the 1930 Act dropped the words 'take away abridge or', but made no other change. It retained the word 'light'.

(c)   Section 54 of the 1939 Act made no change, except to substitute 'right' for 'light'. The resulting nonsense suggests that this was a simple error.

(d)   The Act has unfortunately repeated the error of 1939.

In view of this history, it is submitted that the court's power to correct obvious misprints in a statute[4] enables 'right' to be read as 'light'. The subsection then gives the adjoining owner a right to insist on retaining or restoring windows, or other physical features of the wall (eg eaves with an established right of eavesdrop). If the word 'right' has to remain, it may be possible to support the same result by the word 'things' alone.

15.4   RIGHT TO LIGHT

The right to light is an easement, capable of being acquired by grant or prescription. It is acquired in favour of buildings, and cannot exist in favour of land in its unbuilt state. The basic measure of light to which a building is entitled is that which is sufficient for the ordinary use of the building.[5] The test of an infringement, therefore, is not how much light was taken away by the obstruction in question, but whether sufficient is left for ordinary enjoyment of the dominant premises.

Section 9(a) of the Act specifically protects easements of light. It is clear, therefore, that for example the right to raise a party wall under s 2(1)(l) could not be used so as to interfere with an existing easement of light. The need to protect easements of light may involve the surveyors in difficult questions of law.

(a) It may be doubtful whether there is any easement. If the origin is prescriptive, 20 years' enjoyment provides a starting point, but the law of prescription relating to rights of light is notoriously complex and capricious.[6] Often, rights of light are regulated between neighbours by deeds whose precise legal effect is unclear. They may grant easements, expressly or by implication, but it is quite usual for them to operate only by covenants. Only easements are protected by s 9(a).

(b) If there was once an easement, it may be claimed that it has come to an end by, for example, abandonment. This is another difficult question. Even the bricking up of a window may not amount to abandonment of the easement: there must be evidence of an intention to abandon the right permanently.[7]

The surveyors making an award may therefore have to determine difficult questions of law. It is submitted that it is within their discretion to take their own

---

4 See *R v Wilcock* (1845) 7 QB 317; *Eton College v Minister of Agriculture Fisheries and Food* [1964] Ch 274.
5 *Colls v Home and Colonial Stores Ltd* [1904] AC 179.
6 See Megarry and Wade, *Law of Real Property*, 6th edn (Sweet & Maxwell, 1995).
7 Compare *Tapling v Jones* (1865) 11 HLC 290; *News of the World Ltd v Allen Fairhead & Sons Ltd* [1931] 2 Ch 402; *Marine & General Mutual Life Assurance Society v St James' Real Estate Co Ltd* [1991] 2 EGLR 178.

legal advice on such questions, and that the costs of such advice will fall within
s 10(13).[8]

15.5   RIGHT OF SUPPORT

There is no natural right to the support of a building, but a right may be
acquired by grant or prescription.[9] The right can be acquired by 20 years' user
as of right. Thus a building can acquire the right of support from an adjoining
building provided such support has been enjoyed for at least 20 years. Where
two buildings are in common ownership, and one of them is sold off, the
purchaser will normally acquire a right of support under s 62 of the Law of
Property Act 1925. It appears that it is not an interference with the right of
support to withdraw water from the foundations of the building supported.[10]
However, where the demolition of the neighbouring house caused shrinkage
to the clay underlying the foundation of the plaintiff's house this was held
actionable.[11] Withdrawal of support is only actionable once damage occurs.[12]

Work carried out pursuant to s 2 of the Act clearly includes acts which would
ordinarily be an interference with rights of support. The execution of such
work is expressly authorised by the Act, but liability to make good damage
caused by the work is expressly imposed by various provisions of the Act, in
particular ss 2(3)(a), (4)(a), (5), (6) and 7(2), and the adjoining owner whose
right of support is affected by work carried out under the Act is protected by
these provisions. If there is a dispute, an award made under s 10 will make
provision for the carrying out of such works as are necessary to ensure that the
adjoining owner's property is adequately supported. A question arises as to the
effect of the work on the right of support. Does the right continue, or does the
carrying out of the work, resulting in the adjoining owner's property being
supported by a new structure, mean that the previously enjoyed easement
comes to an end? What is the effect of s 9(a) here? There are two apparently
conflicting authorities to be considered.

(a) In *Selby v Whitbread & Co*,[13] an award authorised the defendant to take
     down a building, thereby removing support from the flank wall of the
     plaintiff's building. A second award required the defendant to support the
     flank wall (validly, it was held) by erecting a substantial pier, but this was
     not done. The plaintiff sued, inter alia, for wrongful withdrawal of support.
     McCardie J rejected this claim, holding that the statutory rights

---

8 See para **11.5**.

9 *Dalton v Angus* (1881) 6 App Cas 740.

10 *Langbrook Properties Ltd v Surrey County Council* [1970] 1 WLR 161.

11 *Brace v South East Regional Housing Association Ltd and Another* [1984] 1 EGLR 144, CA.

12 *Midland Bank Plc v Bardgrove Property Services Ltd and John Willmott (WB)* [1992] 2 EGLR 168,
   CA.

13 [1917] 1 KB 736.

superseded the common law right of support, but he nevertheless granted damages for failure to build the pier. Despite the width of the judge's words (at p 752) about the statute 'repealing' the common law, this decision is not inconsistent with the analysis suggested above (para **15.3.1**). The first award authorised the removal of support, and thereby necessarily overrode the existing right of support to that extent. The upholding of the second award demonstrates that the adjoining owner's principal protection lies in securing adequate provision for continuing support in the award. The fact that the pier had not been built meant that no question could arise as to whether the plaintiff had a right of support from it. It is submitted that the force of s 9(a) is that he would have had such a right as soon as the pier was built, without having to prescribe for it afresh.

(b) In *Brace v South East Regional Housing Association Limited and Another*,[14] the Court of Appeal held that the plaintiff's existing right of support was not determined by an agreement allowing the defendant to demolish the adjoining house. The conflict with the *Selby* decision, however, is superficial. The agreement, although modelled on an award under the 1939 Act, was not an award, and indeed the Act did not apply. The only relevant question before the court was whether the plaintiff had abandoned her right of support, and as a matter of construction of the agreement it was held that she had not. The decision casts no light on the effect of s 9(a).

15.6 PROTECTION FROM THE WEATHER

At common law, there is no easement of protection from the weather, and it follows that a building owner is entitled to remove his building notwithstanding that the effect of this is to expose his neighbour's external wall to the full blast of the elements.[15] But this does not justify the removal of the building owner's building if an internal party wall thereby becomes for the first time exposed to the weather.[16] Further, it has been held that an award can validly impose on the building owner an obligation to maintain a party wall after completion of the initial works, thereby requiring the building owner in effect to keep the party wall weatherproof.[17]

---

14 [1984] 1 EGLR 144.

15 *Phipps v Pears* [1965] 1 QB 76.

16 See *Bradburn v Lindsay* [1983] 2 All ER 408.

17 See *Marchant v Capital & Counties Plc* [1983] 2 EGLR 156, a decision reached by the Court of Appeal notwithstanding the earlier decision in *Leadbetter v Marylebone Corporation* [1904] 2 KB 893, CA.

15.7   NUISANCE

The execution of building work may constitute a nuisance to adjoining or nearby occupiers, by the creation of excessive noise, vibration and dust which disturbs the reasonable enjoyment by such occupiers of their premises. Liability attaches to the person creating the nuisance, and to his employer, if the act done is one which in its very nature involved a special danger of nuisance.[18] In the case of physical damage to property, all damage is actionable. But no cause of action arises in respect of operations insofar as they cause disturbance through noise, if the works are carried on reasonably and all reasonable and proper steps are taken to ensure that no undue inconvenience is caused to neighbours.[19] How far is a building owner vulnerable to this common law claim?

15.7.1   Adjoining owners and occupiers

The Act authorises works which may constitute a nuisance, but it gives adjoining owners the protection of the elaborate machinery for producing an award, and gives adjoining owners and occupiers statutory causes of action for unnecessary inconvenience (s 7(1)) and compensation for loss or damage (s 7(2)).[20] In these circumstances, it is submitted that there is no room for the common law action of nuisance.[21] Nor is there any need if the analysis of those sections in Chapter 6 is correct. The award will be so framed as to minimise interference with the adjoining owner, and his statutory claim under s 7(1) will impose the criterion of unnecessary inconvenience, which must be stricter than the common law test of unreasonable interference with enjoyment. The statutory claim for compensation under s 7(2) will not be narrower than the common law claim for damages.

The previous paragraph applies only to works executed under ss 1 and 2. It does not apply to work executed under s 6, since s 6(10) expressly saves existing liabilities, which must include liability for nuisance,[22] in respect of such work. Here, therefore, adjoining owners and occupiers retain their cause of action in nuisance as well as their statutory causes of action under s 7.

15.7.2   Third parties

The Act does nothing to deprive third parties of their common law rights. Anyone not within the definitions of adjoining owner and adjoining occupier can sue the building owner in nuisance.

---

18 *Matania v National Provincial Bank Ltd* [1936] 2 All ER 633, CA.
19 *Andreae v Selfridge & Co Ltd* [1937] 3 All ER 255, CA.
20 See Chapter 6.
21 Compare *Allen v Gulf Oil Refining Ltd* [1981] AC 1001.
22 It is assumed that 'injury' in s 6(10) is not confined to physical injury, but includes all kinds of legal damage.

15.8   NEGLIGENCE

The mere undertaking of work authorised by the Act cannot constitute negligence. But the Act does not affect any cause of action for negligence in executing such work. The Act does nothing to relieve the building owner of his duty of care, which is non-delegable.[23] Nor does it authorise work to be carried out carelessly.

15.9   TRESPASS

The Act authorises the carrying out of work that would otherwise constitute a trespass, and further confers express rights of entry (s 8). Insofar as the procedures laid down by the Act are followed, no claim for trespass can arise. However, if entry is desired for purposes not related to work authorised by the Act, recourse must be had to the Access to Neighbouring Land Act 1992.

15.10   ACCESS TO NEIGHBOURING LAND ACT 1992 ('THE 1992 ACT')

As has been seen, it was claimed during the passage of the Bill that the provisions of the Act dovetail with the 1992 Act (see para **15.1**). The 1992 Act was passed to remedy the problem which arises where a building stands on or close to a boundary, and it becomes necessary to carry out work to the building that cannot be carried out without access to the neighbouring land, permission for which is refused.

The 1992 Act enables the court to make an 'access order' if and only if it is satisfied:

(a)   that the works are reasonably necessary for the preservation of the whole or any part of the dominant land (ie the building owner's land, to use the 1996 Act's terminology); and

(b)   that they cannot be carried out, or would be substantially more difficult to carry out, without the entry upon the servient land (ie the adjoining owner's land).[24]

Certain works ('basic preservation works') are automatically considered to be reasonably necessary for the preservation of the land. The basic preservation works are:

(a)   maintenance, repair or renewal of any part of a building or other structure comprised in or situate on the dominant land;

---

23 See *Hughes v Percival* (1883) 8 App Cas 443.
24 See s 1(2).

(b) the clearance, repair or renewal of any drain, sewer, pipe or cable so comprised or situate;

(c) the treatment, cutting back, felling, removal or replacement of any hedge, tree, shrub or other growing thing which is so comprised and which is or is in danger of becoming damaged, diseased, dangerous, insecurely rooted, or dead;

(d) the filling in, or clearance, of any ditch so comprised.[25]

Section 2 of the 1992 Act enables the court to settle the terms of an access order, including terms for regulating the time and manner of execution of the work, and provision for compensation for loss suffered by the owner of the servient land. The access order may also (s 2(5)) require the applicant to pay the respondent a sum for the privilege of entering the servient land, calculated by reference to the financial advantage of the order to the applicant and connected persons, and the degree of inconvenience likely to be caused to the respondent or other person by the entry. This, however, does not apply where the application relates to residential land.

In general, the 1992 Act and the Act will not overlap, because the 1992 Act only applies where work is required to be done to the dominant land, whereas an essential feature of the rights conferred by the Act is that they include the right to do work to the adjoining owner's part of a party wall. Although works under s 2 of the Act may, insofar as they affect the building owner's land, constitute works to the dominant land under the 1992 Act, an access order under the 1992 Act will be of no utility, since such an order cannot authorise works to the servient owner's land, ie to the adjoining owner's part of the party wall.

However, situations may arise where the building owner wishes not only to carry out work under the Act, but also to carry out further work to parts of his building which are not party walls, and for that purpose requires access to the adjoining owner's land. The rights of entry given by the Act do not extend to work falling outside the scope of the Act. In some circumstances it may be advantageous for the building owner, therefore, to consider whether he should also proceed by way of application under the 1992 Act, in order to obtain authority simultaneously to carry out further works of that kind. But given the somewhat elaborate provisions regarding access orders in the 1992 Act, and the fact that such an order can only be obtained on application to the court, this course will rarely be of practical utility.

15.11   OTHER STATUTORY REQUIREMENTS

An award cannot require work not permitted by the general law (s 7(5)(a)). For example, it could not require that building work be carried out without

---

25 See s 1(4).

complying with appropriate safety requirements, or using materials not permitted by the building regulations. Difficulties may, however, sometimes arise where it appears to the surveyors desirable that the work proposed by the building owner be carried out in a modified way for technical reasons, where this may necessitate a further application for planning permission or listed building consent, or relaxation of building regulations, under the powers conferred by the Building Act 1984 on local authorities. It is submitted that under s 10(12) the surveyors have power in an award to regulate the carrying out of work in such a way that further statutory consents may be necessary, and are not restricted by the terms (or absence) of permissions and approvals obtained by the building owner at the time the award comes to be made. Otherwise, the surveyors might be forced into a position where they had to choose between approving works which they considered unduly injurious to the adjoining owner, and refusing to approve any works. However, it is submitted that they ought to take the step of making an award that requires further approval only where this is necessary to ensure fairness.

Nothing in the Act affects the need for planning permission and (where appropriate) listed building consent under the Town and Country Planning Act 1990 and the Planning (Listed Buildings and Conservation Areas) Act 1990. Nor does the Act affect the requirements of building regulations or the regulations concerning work on construction sites.

Chapter 16

CRIMINAL OFFENCES

16.1 SECTION 16(1): REFUSAL OF ENTRY

Section 16 of the Act creates two criminal offences. First, under s 16(1), if an occupier of land or premises refuses to permit a person to do anything which he is entitled to do with regard to the land or premises under s 8(1) or (5) he commits an offence. Section 8(1) is the provision which entitles a building owner to enter and remain on any land or premises for the purpose of executing any work in pursuance of the Act. Section 8(5) is the provision entitling a surveyor appointed or selected under s 10 of the Act to enter or remain on any land or premises for the purpose of carrying out the object for which he is appointed or selected.

16.2 VICARIOUS LIABILITY

The offence can only be committed by an occupier. The occupier can be vicariously liable for acts committed by his servants or agents, and, indeed, if the occupier is a corporation, it can only act through its servants or agents. The principles of criminal liability of corporations for the acts of their servants or agents are well established.

The act or default of a subordinate employee who is not part of the controlling mind or will of the corporation will not make the corporation liable (unless the subordinate employee is following instructions given by the controlling mind or will).[1] It follows that a corporate occupier will only be liable to conviction if the refusal emanates either from those who control the mind and will of the corporation, such as directors, or from subordinate employees acting on their instructions.

It is an essential ingredient of the offence under s 16(1) that the occupier knows or has reasonable cause to believe that the person concerned is entitled to enter the land or carry out the work (s 16(1)(b)). In the case of a corporation the relevant knowledge or reasonable cause to believe will be that of a servant or agent. The guilty mind of a director or manager would render the corporation itself guilty, but not necessarily that of a subordinate employee who is not in a managerial position.[2]

---

1 *Tesco Supermarkets Ltd v Nattrass* [1971] 2 All ER 127, HL; *R v British Steel Plc* [1995] 1 WLR 1356, CA.

2 See *Director of Public Prosecutions v Kent and Sussex Contractors Ltd* [1944] 1 All ER 119; *R v ICR Haulage* [1944] 1 All ER 691; *John Henshall Quarries v Harvey* [1965] 1 All ER 725.

16.3   REFUSAL

The offence involves a refusal to permit entry etc. What amounts to refusal will be a question of fact. It is submitted that there will not be a refusal in, inter alia, the following circumstances.

(a) Excluding the person requiring entry from the land for sufficient time to verify his identity and business. It is submitted that it is incumbent on the person requiring entry to demonstrate to the occupier that he has a prima facie right to do so, and until this is done there is no refusal.[3] It follows that it would be prudent for persons seeking to exercise their rights to make an appointment with the occupier and to establish their credentials and to agree times for subsequent visits.

(b) Where the person seeking admittance is kept waiting for a short period.

(c) Where the occupier remonstrates with the person seeking admittance, but without refusing entry.[4]

(d) Where the occupier simply fails to make access available, for example because no-one is at the premises when the person seeking entry calls. Mere inaction or failure to give entry is not the same as refusal.[5]

16.4   REASONABLE CAUSE

The words 'has reasonable cause to believe' clearly involve something less than knowledge. Probably, the words are intended to import the idea of the occupier being in possession of information from which a reasonable person in his position would believe that the person is so entitled. The test is no doubt objective: does the occupier have material which viewed objectively would give a reasonable person grounds for believing that the person claiming entry was entitled to that right? For this reason, a notice of entry under s 8 should explicitly state the entitlement of the person entering.[6]

16.5   ENTRY PURSUANT TO THE ACT

The offence is only committed where rights of entry pursuant to the Act are being exercised. If, therefore, the statutory procedures have not been followed, or a purported award is a nullity, refusal to permit entry would not constitute an offence, because no rights under the Act will have been conferred. For

---

3 Compare *Duncan v Dowding* [1897] 1 QB 575.
4 Compare *Caswell v Worcestershire Justices* (1889) 53 JP 820.
5 Compare *Lowson v Percy Main & District Social Club & Institute* [1979] ICR 568.
6 See Appendix 4, Precedent 7.

example, an attempt by a surveyor to exercise rights under s 8(5) which is the subject of a refusal will not give rise to an offence if he has not been properly appointed under s 10.

16.6 OCCUPIERS

The term 'occupier' is not defined by the Act, although s 20 defines 'adjoining occupier', without defining occupation. It is not thought that any useful inference can be derived from the definition of 'owner', nor from extraneous fields such as rating.[7]

There appears to be no reason to exclude any person who maintains sufficient presence on the land to enable him to frustrate the statutory right of entry. It is submitted that the offence can be committed not only by owner-occupiers, and tenants, but also by licensees and even squatters.

16.7 SECTION 16(2): HINDERING ENTRY

Section 16(2) of the Act creates an offence of hindering or obstructing a person exercising rights under s 8(1) or (5). It is not provided that the acts complained of must amount to physical restraint, and it seems that verbal abuse or other intimidation could be sufficient to constitute the offence. It is, however, submitted that the acts complained of must be accompanied by the necessary criminal intent. Although s 16(2) does not use the word 'intentionally',[8] it is well established that, in general, proof of mens rea is required for a criminal offence. Accordingly, acts done without an intention to hinder or obstruct will not constitute an offence, even if they in fact have that effect.

It is further submitted that mere inaction will not constitute the offence. If, for example, access to the premises can only be gained in a dangerous and difficult way, the occupier will not be liable for failing to make the access safe.[9]

16.8 PROCEDURE

The offences created by s 16 are summary offences, and can only be tried in the magistrates' court. They cannot be the subject of imprisonment. The reference to a fine of level 3 on the standard scale is to the scale fixed pursuant to s 37 of the Criminal Justice Act 1982 as amended by s 17 of the Criminal Justice Act 1991.

---

7 But see *Northern Ireland Commissioner of Valuation v Fermanagh Protestant Board of Education*
  [1969] 3 All ER 352; *Trustees of Methodist Schools v O'Leary* (1993) 25 HLR 364.

8 Contrast, for example, the Banking Act 1987, s 40(3).

9 Compare *R v Ahmad (Zafar)* (1987) 84 Cr App R 64, CA, (1986) 18 HLR 416.

Both offences are of a continuing nature for the purposes of the 6-month time-limit for laying informations under the Magistrates' Court Act 1980, s 127.[10]

---

10 Compare *Camden London Borough Council v Marshall* [1996] EGCS 104.

Appendix 1

PARTY WALL ETC ACT 1996

(1996 c 40)

ARRANGEMENT OF SECTIONS

Construction and repair of walls on line of junction

An Act to make provision in respect of party walls, and excavation and construction in proximity to certain buildings or structures; and for connected purposes.

[18th July 1996]

Construction and repair of walls on line of junction

1   New building on line of junction

(1) This section shall have effect where lands of different owners adjoin and—

- (a)   are not built on at the line of junction; or
- (b)   are built on at the line of junction only to the extent of a boundary wall (not being a party fence wall or the external wall of a building),

and either owner is about to build on any part of the line of junction.

(2) If a building owner desires to build a party wall or party fence wall on the line of junction he shall, at least one month before he intends the building work to start, serve on any adjoining owner a notice which indicates his desire to build and describes the intended wall.

(3) If, having been served with notice described in subsection (2), an adjoining owner serves on the building owner a notice indicating his consent to the building of a party wall or party fence wall—

- (a)   the wall shall be built half on the land of each of the two owners or in such other position as may be agreed between the two owners; and
- (b)   the expense of building the wall shall be from time to time defrayed by the two owners in such proportion as has regard to the use made or to be made of the wall by each of them and to the cost of labour and materials prevailing at the time when that use is made by each owner respectively.

(4) If, having been served with notice described in subsection (2), an adjoining owner does not consent under this subsection to the building of a party wall or party fence wall, the building owner may only build the wall—

- (a)   at his own expense; and
- (b)   as an external wall or a fence wall, as the case may be, placed wholly on his own land,

and consent under this subsection is consent by a notice served within the period of fourteen days beginning with the day on which the notice described in subsection (2) is served.

(5) If the building owner desires to build on the line of junction a wall placed wholly on his own land he shall, at least one month before he intends the building work to start, serve on any adjoining owner a notice which indicates his desire to build and describes the intended wall.

(6) Where the building owner builds a wall wholly on his own land in accordance with subsection (4) or (5) he shall have the right, at any time in the period which—

(a) begins one month after the day on which the notice mentioned in the subsection concerned was served, and
(b) ends twelve months after that day,

to place below the level of the land of the adjoining owner such projecting footings and foundations as are necessary for the construction of the wall.

(7) Where the building owner builds a wall wholly on his own land in accordance with subsection (4) or (5) he shall do so at his own expense and shall compensate any adjoining owner and any adjoining occupier for any damage to his property occasioned by—

(a) the building of the wall;
(b) the placing of any footings or foundations placed in accordance with subsection (6).

(8) Where any dispute arises under this section between the building owner and any adjoining owner or occupier it is to be determined in accordance with section 10.

Commentary in text—paragraphs **3.2–3.5**.

This section applies where there is no existing building on the boundary. It corresponds to s 45(1) of the 1939 Act.

Section 1(1)(b)—This adds the case where only projecting footings are built on the boundary.

Section 1(2)—If the building owner intends to build astride the boundary, he must serve notice under this section. If he intends to build wholly on his side of the boundary, except for projecting footings or foundations, he must serve notice under s 1(5).

Section 1(3)—This sets out the automatic consequences of consent by the adjoining owner.

Section 1(4)—The requirement for consent under this subsection to be given within 14 days is new. It is not clear why it does not apply for the purposes of s 1(3) as well (see para **3.3.4**).

Section 1(6)—Either notice will entitle the building owner to place footings or foundations in the adjoining owner's land, subject to the conditions in s 1(7). The time-limit for such works has been extended by 6 months.

Section 1(8)—In contrast to s 2, no dispute arises automatically for lack of consent. The building owner may be content to build wholly on his own land.

---

2   Repair etc. of party wall: rights of owner

(1) This section applies where lands of different owners adjoin and at the line of junction the said lands are built on or a boundary wall, being a party fence wall or the external wall of a building, has been erected.

(2) A building owner shall have the following rights—

(a) to underpin, thicken or raise a party structure, a party fence wall, or an external wall which belongs to the building owner and is built against a party structure or party fence wall;

(b) to make good, repair, or demolish and rebuild, a party structure or party fence wall in a case where such work is necessary on account of defect or want of repair of the structure or wall;

(c) to demolish a partition which separates buildings belonging to different owners but does not conform with statutory requirements and to build instead a party wall which does so conform;

(d) in the case of buildings connected by arches or structures over public ways or over passages belonging to other persons, to demolish the whole or part of such buildings, arches or structures which do not conform with statutory requirements and to rebuild them so that they do so conform;

(e) to demolish a party structure which is of insufficient strength or height for the purposes of any intended building of the building owner and to rebuild it of sufficient strength or height for the said purposes (including rebuilding to a lesser height or thickness where the rebuilt structure is of sufficient strength and height for the purposes of any adjoining owner);

(f) to cut into a party structure for any purpose (which may be or include the purpose of inserting a damp proof course);

(g) to cut away from a party wall, party fence wall, external wall or boundary wall any footing or any projecting chimney breast, jamb or flue, or other projection on or over the land of the building owner in order to erect, raise or underpin any such wall or for any other purpose;

(h) to cut away or demolish parts of any wall or building of an adjoining owner overhanging the land of the building owner or overhanging a party wall, to the extent that it is necessary to cut away or demolish the parts to enable a vertical wall to be erected or raised against the wall or building of the adjoining owner;

(j) to cut into the wall of an adjoining owner's building in order to insert a flashing or other weather-proofing of a wall erected against that wall;

(k) to execute any other necessary works incidental to the connection of a party structure with the premises adjoining it;

(l) to raise a party fence wall, or to raise such a wall for use as a party wall, and to demolish a party fence wall and rebuild it as a party fence wall or as a party wall;

(m) subject to the provisions of section 11(7), to reduce, or to demolish and rebuild, a party wall or party fence wall to—

    (i) a height of not less than two metres where the wall is not used by an adjoining owner to any greater extent than a boundary wall; or

    (ii) a height currently enclosed upon by the building of an adjoining owner;

(n) to expose a party wall or party structure hitherto enclosed subject to providing adequate weathering.

(3) Where work mentioned in paragraph (a) of subsection (2) is not necessary on account of defect or want of repair of the structure or wall concerned, the right falling within that paragraph is exercisable—

(a) subject to making good all damage occasioned by the work to the adjoining premises or to their internal furnishings and decorations; and

(b) where the work is to a party structure or external wall, subject to carrying any relevant flues and chimney stacks up to such a height and in such materials as may be agreed between the building owner and the adjoining owner concerned or, in the event of dispute, determined in accordance with section 10;

and relevant flues and chimney stacks are those which belong to an adjoining owner and either form part of or rest on or against the party structure or external wall.

(4) The right falling within subsection (2)(e) is exercisable subject to—

(a) making good all damage occasioned by the work to the adjoining premises or to their internal furnishings and decorations; and

(b) carrying any relevant flues and chimney stacks up to such a height and in such materials as may be agreed between the building owner and the adjoining owner concerned or, in the event of dispute, determined in accordance with section 10;

and relevant flues and chimney stacks are those which belong to an adjoining owner and either form part of or rest on or against the party structure.

(5) Any right falling within subsection (2)(f), (g) or (h) is exercisable subject to making good all damage occasioned by the work to the adjoining premises or to their internal furnishings and decorations.

(6) The right falling within subsection (2)(j) is exercisable subject to making good all damage occasioned by the work to the wall of the adjoining owner's building.

(7) The right falling within subsection (2)(m) is exercisable subject to—

(a) reconstructing any parapet or replacing an existing parapet with another one; or

(b)   constructing a parapet where one is needed but did not exist before.

(8) For the purposes of this section a building or structure which was erected before the day on which this Act was passed shall be deemed to conform with statutory requirements if it conforms with the statutes regulating buildings or structures on the date on which it was erected.

Commentary in text—paragraphs **3.6–3.7**.

This section applies where there is already an existing building on the boundary. It corresponds to s 46 of the 1939 Act.

A party structure notice must be served under s 3 before the rights conferred by this section can be exercised. The adjoining owner can then serve a counter-notice under s 4. Unless one of these notices is expressly consented to, there will then be a dispute which must be resolved under s 10 (s 5).

For the difference between these rights and common law rights see *Standard Bank of British South America v Stokes* (1878) 9 Ch D 68; *Selby v Whitbread & Co* [1917] 1 KB 736

Section (2)(a), (b), (e), (m)—Special provision for the cost of works within these subsections is made in s 11(4), (5), (6), (7) respectively.

---

3   Party structure notices

(1) Before exercising any right conferred on him by section 2 a building owner shall serve on any adjoining owner a notice (in this Act referred to as a 'party structure notice') stating—

(a)   the name and address of the building owner;
(b)   the nature and particulars of the proposd work including, in cases where the building owner proposes to construct special foundations, plans, sections and details of construction of the special foundations together with reasonable particulars of the loads to be carried thereby; and
(c)   the date on which the proposed work will begin.

(2) A party structure notice shall—

(a)   be served at least two months before the date on which the proposed work will begin;
(b)   cease to have effect if the work to which it relates—
   (i)   has not begun within the period of twelve months beginning with the day on which the notice is served; and
   (ii) is not prosecuted with due diligence.

(3) Nothing in this section shall—

(a)   prevent a building owner from exercising with the consent in writing of the adjoining owners and of the adjoining occupiers any right conferred on him by section 2; or

(b) require a building owner to serve any party structure notice before complying with any notice served under any statutory provisions relating to dangerous or neglected structures.

Commentary in text—paragraph **3.8**.

This section requires the service of a party structure notice before any right under s 2 is exercised. It corresponds to s 47 of the 1939 Act.

Section 3(2)(b)—This time-limit has been extended by 6 months. It will not apply where a dispute is referred under s 10, and the award is not made within the time-limit (see *Leadbetter v Marylebone Corp* [1905] 1 KB 661).

Section 3(3)(a)—If all adjoining owners and occupiers consent in writing to his proposals, the building owner need not serve a party structure notice.

Section 3(3)(b)—The statutory provisions were formerly limited to Part VII of the 1939 Act, but will now also include relevant provisions under, for example, the Building Act 1984. This dispensation applies only to work required by the notice served on the building owner: additional work requires a party structure notice (see *Spiers and Son Ltd v Troup* (1915) 84 LJKB 1986).

---

4 Counter notices

(1) An adjoining owner may, having been served with a party structure notice serve on the building owner a notice (in this Act referred to as a 'counter notice') setting out—

(a) in respect of a party fence wall or party structure, a requirement that the building owner build in or on the wall or structure to which the notice relates such chimney copings, breasts, jambs or flues, or such piers or recesses or other like works, as may reasonably be required for the convenience of the adjoining owner;

(b) in respect of special foundations to which the adjoining owner consents under section 7(4) below, a requirement that the special foundations—

　(i) be placed at a specified greater depth than that proposed by the building owner; or

　(ii) be constructed of sufficient strength to bear the load to be carried by columns of any intended building of the adjoining owner, or both.

(2) A counter notice shall—

(a) specify the works required by the notice to be executed and shall be accompanied by plans, sections and particulars of such works; and

(b) be served within the period of one month beginning with the day on which the party structure notice is served.

(3) A building owner on whom a counter notice has been served shall comply with the requirements of the counter notice unless the execution of the works required by the counter notice would—

(a) be injurious to him;

(b) cause unnecessary inconvenience to him; or

(c) cause unnecessary delay in the execution of the works pursuant to the party structure notice.

Commentary in text—paragraph **3.9**.

This section enables the adjoining owner to serve a counter-notice in response to a party structure notice, requiring modifications to the building owner's proposals. It corresponds to s 48 of the 1939 Act.

The adjoining owner must pay the costs of the works he requires (s 11(9)), and may have to give security for such costs (s 12(2)).

Section 4(1)(b)—For 'special foundations' see s 20. Section 7(4) prohibits special foundations unless the adjoining owner consents. This section enables him to consent subject to modifications.

---

5   Disputes arising under sections 3 and 4

If an owner on whom a party structure notice or a counter notice has been served does not serve a notice indicating his consent to it within the period of fourteen days beginning with the day on which the party structure notice or counter notice was served, he shall be deemed to have dissented from the notice and a dispute shall be deemed to have arisen between the parties.

Commentary in text—paragraph **3.10**.

This section provides that, in default of express consent, any notice under s 3 or 4 constitutes a dispute which must be resolved under s 10. It corresponds to s 49 of the 1939 Act.

Adjacent excavation and construction

6   Adjacent excavation and construction

(1) This section applies where—

(a) a building owner proposes to excavate, or excavate for and erect a building or structure, within a distance of three metres measured horizontally from any part of a building or structure of an adjoining owner; and

(b) any part of the proposed excavation, building or structure will within those three metres extend to a lower level than the level of the bottom of the foundations of the building or structure of the adjoining owner.

(2) This section also applies where—

(a) a building owner proposes to excavate, or excavate for and erect a building or structure, within a distance of six metres measured horizontally from any part of a building or structure of an adjoining owner; and

(b) any part of the proposed excavation, building or structure will within those six metres meet a plane drawn downwards in the direction of the excavation, building or structure of the building owner at an angle of forty-five degrees to the horizontal from the line formed by the intersection of the plane of the level of the bottom of the foundations of the building or structure of the adjoining owner with the plane of the external face of the external wall of the building or structure of the adjoining owner.

(3) The building owner may, and if required by the adjoining owner shall, at his own expense underpin or otherwise strengthen or safeguard the foundations of the building or structure of the adjoining owner so far as may be necessary.

(4) Where the buildings or structures of different owners are within the respective distances mentioned in subsections (1) and (2) the owners of those buildings or structures shall be deemed to be adjoining owners for the purposes of this section.

(5) In any case where this section applies the building owner shall, at least one month before beginning to excavate, or excavate for and erect a building or structure, serve on the adjoining owner a notice indicating his proposals and stating whether he proposes to underpin or otherwise strengthen or safeguard the foundations of the building or structure of the adjoining owner.

(6) The notice referred to in subsection (5) shall be accompanied by plans and sections showing—

(a) the site and depth of any excavation the building owner proposes to make;
(b) if he proposes to erect a building or structure, its site.

(7) If an owner on whom a notice referred to in subsection (5) has been served does not serve a notice indicating his consent to it within the period of fourteen days beginning with the day on which the notice referred to in subsection (5) was served, he shall be deemed to have dissented from the notice and a dispute shall be deemed to have arisen between the parties.

(8) The notice referred to in subsection (5) shall cease to have effect if the work to which the notice relates—

(a) has not begun within the period of twelve months beginning with the day on which the notice was served; and
(b) is not prosecuted with due diligence.

(9) On completion of any work executed in pursuance of this section the building owner shall if so requested by the adjoining owner supply him with particulars including plans and sections of the work.

(10) Nothing in this section shall relieve the building owner from any liability to which he would otherwise be subject for injury to any adjoining owner or any adjoining occupier by reason of work executed by him.

Commentary in text—Chapter 4.

This section restricts the building owner's right to excavate his own land within 3 or 6 metres of buildings of adjoining owners. It corresponds to s 50 of the 1939 Act.

Section 6(3)—Where the section applies, the building owner has a right to underpin, or otherwise safeguard, adjoining buildings, and an obligation to do so if the adjoining owner requires. In either case, the building owner must pay the expenses.

Section 6(5)—The building owner must serve a notice with similar consequences to a party structure notice, except that there is no provision for a counter-notice by the adjoining owner.

Section 6(10)—The building owner's potential common law liabilities include vicarious liability in negligence for his independent contractor (see *Hughes v Percival* (1883) 8 App Cas 443), and nuisance by withdrawal of support (see *Brace v South East Regional Housing Association Ltd and Another* [1984] 1 EGLR 144, CA). It is thought that 'injury' is not restricted to physical injury (see para **15.7.1**).

Rights etc.

7   Compensation etc.

(1) A building owner shall not exercise any right conferred on him by this Act in such a manner or at such time as to cause unnecessary inconvenience to any adjoining owner or to any adjoining occupier.

(2) The building owner shall compensate any adjoining owner and any adjoining occupier for any loss or damage which may result to any of them by reason of any work executed in pursuance of this Act.

(3) Where a building owner in exercising any right conferred on him by this Act lays open any part of the adjoining land or building he shall at his own expense make and maintain so long as may be necessary a proper hoarding, shoring or fans or temporary construction for the protection of the adjoining land or building and the security of any adjoining occupier.

(4) Nothing in this Act shall authorise the building owner to place special foundations on land of an adjoining owner without his previous consent in writing.

(5) Any works executed in pursuance of this Act shall—

(a)   comply with the provisions of statutory requirements; and
(b)   be executed in accordance with such plans, sections and particulars as may be agreed between the owners or in the event of dispute determined in accordance with section 10;

and no deviation shall be made from those plans, sections and particulars except such as may be agreed between the owners (or surveyors acting on their behalf) or in the event of dispute determined in accordance with section 10.

Commentary in text—see Chapter 6 and paras **5.3**, **9.9** and **15.7**.

This section imposes miscellaneous conditions on the exercise of the statutory rights. It corresponds to s 51 of the 1939 Act.

Sections 7(1)–(3)—These sections create statutory duties which can be enforced by adjoining owners and occupiers. They are the only protection which the Act provides for adjoining occupiers.

Section 7(1)—This section applies to the carrying out of the works. It imposes liability for unreasonable delay: see *Jolliffe v Woodhouse* (1894) 10 TLR 553.

Section 7(2)—This section applies to the effect of the completed works. It is a new provision, overruling *Adams v Marylebone BC* [1907] 2 KB 822.

Section 7(3)—See also ss 2(2)(e) and 11(6).

Section 7(4)—This is the general principle relating to special foundations.

Section 7(5)—This is part of the essential machinery for ensuring that only works permitted (a) by law, and (b) by an award, will be carried out under the Act.

---

8   Rights of entry

(1) A building owner, his servants, agents and workmen may during usual working hours enter and remain on any land or premises for the purpose of executing any work in pursuance of this Act and may remove any furniture or fittings or take any other action necessary for that purpose.

(2) If the premises are closed, the building owner, his agents and workmen may, if accompanied by a constable or other police officer, break open any fences or doors in order to enter the premises.

(3) No land or premises may be entered by any person under subsection (1) unless the building owner serves on the owner and the occupier of the land or premises—

(a)   in case of emergency, such notice of the intention to enter as may be reasonably practicable;

(b)   in any other case, such notice of the intention to enter as complies with subsection (4).

(4) Notice complies with this subsection if it is served in a period of not less than fourteen days ending with the day of the proposed entry.

(5) A surveyor appointed or selected under section 10 may during usual working hours enter and remain on any land or premises for the purpose of carrying out the object for which he is appointed or selected.

(6) No land or premises may be entered by a surveyor under subsection (5) unless the building owner who is a party to the dispute concerned serves on the owner and the occupier of the land or premises—

(a)   in case of emergency, such notice of the intention to enter as may be reasonably practicable;

(b)   in any other case, such notice of the intention to enter as complies with subsection (4).

Commentary in text—Chapter 7.

This section gives conditional rights of entry for the purpose of exercising the statutory rights. It corresponds to s 53 of the 1939 Act. It is perhaps arguable that they are registrable as equitable easements (see para **14.3.2**).

Section 8(5)—This right is new.

---

9 Easements
Nothing in this Act shall—

    (a) authorise any interference with an easement of light or other easements in or relating to a party wall; or

    (b) prejudicially affect any right of any person to preserve or restore any right or other thing in or connected with a party wall in case of the party wall being pulled down or rebuilt.

Commentary in text—paragraphs **15.3–15.6**.

This section safeguards existing easements and rights. It corresponds to s 54 of the 1939 Act.

Section 9(a)—An agreement authorising the removal of a supporting wall does not without more abandon the adjoining owner's easement of support (see *Brace v South East Regional Housing Association Ltd and Another* [1984] 1 EGLR 144, CA).

Section 9(b)—It is thought that the second reference to 'right' is a mistake for 'light' which originated in the 1939 Act (see para **15.3.2**).

Resolution of disputes

10 Resolution of disputes
(1) Where a dispute arises or is deemed to have arisen between a building owner and an adjoining owner in respect of any matter connected with any work to which this Act relates either—

    (a) both parties shall concur in the appointment of one surveyor (in this section referred to as an 'agreed surveyor'); or

    (b) each party shall appoint a surveyor and the two surveyors so appointed shall forthwith select a third surveyor (all of whom are in this section referred to as 'the three surveyors').

(2) All appointments and selections made under this section shall be in writing and shall not be rescinded by either party.

(3) If an agreed surveyor—

    (a) refuses to act;

    (b) neglects to act for a period of ten days beginning with the day on which either party serves a request on him;

    (c) dies before the dispute is settled; or

(d)   becomes or deems himself incapable of acting,

the proceedings for settling such dispute shall begin *de novo.*

(4) If either party to the dispute—

(a)   refuses to appoint a surveyor under subsection (1)(b), or

(b)   neglects to appoint a surveyor under subsection (1)(b) for a period of ten days beginning with the day on which the other party serves a request on him,

the other party may make the appointment on his behalf.

(5) If, before the dispute is settled, a surveyor appointed under paragraph (b) of subsection (1) by a party to the dispute dies, or becomes or deems himself incapable of acting, the party who appointed him may appoint another surveyor in his place with the same power and authority.

(6) If a surveyor—

(a)   appointed under paragraph (b) of subsection (1) by a party to the dispute; or

(b)   appointed under subsection (4) or (5),

refuses to act effectively, the surveyor of the other party may proceed to act *ex parte* and anything so done by him shall be as effectual as if he had been an agreed surveyor.

(7) If a surveyor—

(a)   appointed under paragraph (b) of subsection (1) by a party to the dispute; or

(b)   appointed under subsection (4) or (5),

neglects to act effectively for a period of ten days beginning with the day on which either party or the surveyor of the other party serves a request on him, the surveyor of the other party may proceed to act *ex parte* in respect of the subject matter of the request and anything so done by him shall be as effectual as if he had been an agreed surveyor.

(8) If either surveyor appointed under subsection (1)(b) by a party to the dispute refuses to select a third surveyor under subsection (1) or (9), or neglects to do so for a period of ten days beginning with the day on which the other surveyor serves a request on him—

(a)   the appointing officer; or

(b)   in cases where the relevant appointing officer or his employer is a party to the dispute, the Secretary of State,

may on the application of either surveyor select a third surveyor who shall have the same power and authority as if he had been selected under subsection (1) or subsection (9).

(9) If a third surveyor selected under subsection (1)(b)—

(a)   refuses to act;

(b)   neglects to act for a period of ten days beginning with the day on which either party or the surveyor appointed by either party serves a request on him; or

(c)   dies, or becomes or deems himself incapable of acting, before the dispute is settled,

the other two of the three surveyors shall forthwith select another surveyor in his place with the same power and authority.

(10) The agreed surveyor or as the case may be the three surveyors or any two of them shall settle by award any matter—

(a)   which is connected with any work to which this Act relates, and

(b)   which is in dispute between the building owner and the adjoining owner.

(11) Either of the parties or either of the surveyors appointed by the parties may call upon the third surveyor selected in pursuance of this section to determine the disputed matters and he shall make the necessary award.

(12) An award may determine—

(a)   the right to execute any work;

(b)   the time and manner of executing any work; and

(c)   any other matter arising out of or incidental to the dispute including the costs of making the award;

but any period appointed by the award for executing any work shall not unless otherwise agreed between the building owner and the adjoining owner begin to run until after the expiration of the period prescribed by this Act for service of the notice in respect of which the dispute arises or is deemed to have arisen.

(13) The reasonable costs incurred in—

(a)   making or obtaining an award under this section;

(b)   reasonable inspections of work to which the award relates; and

(c)   any other matter arising out of the dispute,

shall be paid by such of the parties as the surveyor or surveyors making the award determine.

(14) Where the surveyors appointed by the parties make an award the surveyors shall serve it forthwith on the parties.

(15) Where an award is made by the third surveyor—

(a)   he shall, after payment of the costs of the award, serve it forthwith on the parties or their appointed surveyors; and

(b)   if it is served on their appointed surveyors, they shall serve it forthwith on the parties.

(16) The award shall be conclusive and shall not except as provided by this section be questioned in any court.

(17) Either of the parties to the dispute may, within the period of fourteen days beginning with the day on which an award made under this section is served on him, appeal to the county court against the award and the county court may—

    (a)   rescind the award or modify it in such manner as the court thinks fit; and

    (b)   make such order as to costs as the court thinks fit.

Commentary in text—Chapters 8, 9.

This section provides the procedure for resolving disputes. It corresponds to s 55 of the 1939 Act. The power to appeal to the High Court has been abolished.

Section 10(12)(c)—An award cannot grant a right to carry out further building works, not presently required, at some time in the future (see *Leadbetter v Marylebone Corp* [1904] 2 KB 893, CA), but it can impose a continuing obligation, for example to maintain (see *Marchant v Capital & Counties Plc* [1983] 2 EGLR 156). An obligation imposed by an award does not run with the land, but remains with the party concerned (see *Selby v Whitbread & Co* [1917] 1 KB 736).

Section 10(16)—An award may be partly void for want of jurisdiction (see *Re Stone and Hastie* [1903] 2 KB 463).

Section 10(17)—The appeal is by way of rehearing (see *Chartered Society of Physiotherapy v Simmonds Church Smiles* [1995] 1 EGLR 155). It will be registrable as a pending land action (see para **14.13.1**).

Expenses

11   Expenses

(1) Except as provided under this section expenses of work under this Act shall be defrayed by the building owner.

(2) Any dispute as to responsibility for expenses shall be settled as provided in section 10.

(3) An expense mentioned in section 1(3)(b) shall be defrayed as there mentioned.

(4) Where work is carried out in exercise of the right mentioned in section 2(2)(a), and the work is necessary on account of defect or want of repair of the structure or wall concerned, the expenses shall be defrayed by the building owner and the adjoining owner in such proportion as has regard to—

    (a)   the use which the owners respectively make or may make of the structure or wall concerned; and

    (b)   responsibility for the defect or want of repair concerned, if more than one owner makes use of the structure or wall concerned.

(5) Where work is carried out in exercise of the right mentioned in section 2(2)(b) the expenses shall be defrayed by the building owner and the adjoining owner in such proportion as has regard to—

(a) the use which the owners respectively make or may make of the structure or wall concerned; and

(b) responsibility for the defect or want of repair concerned, if more than one owner makes use of the structure or wall concerned.

(6) Where the adjoining premises are laid open in exercise of the right mentioned in section 2(2)(e) a fair allowance in respect of disturbance and inconvenience shall be paid by the building owner to the adjoining owner or occupier.

(7) Where a building owner proposes to reduce the height of a party wall or party fence wall under section 2(2)(m) the adjoining owner may serve a counter notice under section 4 requiring the building owner to maintain the existing height of the wall, and in such case the adjoining owner shall pay to the building owner a due proportion of the cost of the wall so far as it exceeds—

(a) two metres in height; or

(b) the height currently enclosed upon by the building of the adjoining owner.

(8) Where the building owner is required to make good damage under this Act the adjoining owner has a right to require that the expenses of such making good be determined in accordance with section 10 and paid to him in lieu of the carrying out of work to make the damage good.

(9) Where—

(a) works are carried out, and

(b) some of the works are carried out at the request of the adjoining owner or in pursuance of a requirement made by him,

he shall defray the expenses of carrying out the works requested or required by him.

(10) Where—

(a) consent in writing has been given to the construction of special foundations on land of an adjoining owner; and

(b) the adjoining owner erects any building or structure and its cost is found to be increased by reason of the existence of the said foundations,

the owner of the building to which the said foundations belong shall, on receiving an account with any necessary invoices and other supporting documents within the period of two months beginning with the day of the completion of the work by the adjoining owner, repay to the adjoining owner so much of the cost as is due to the existence of the said foundations.

(11) Where use is subsequently made by the adjoining owner of work carried out solely at the expense of the building owner the adjoining owner shall pay a

due proportion of the expenses incurred by the building owner in carrying out that work; and for this purpose he shall be taken to have incurred expenses calculated by reference to what the cost of the work would be if it were carried out at the time when that subsequent use is made.

Commentary in text—Chapter 11.

This section makes provision for allocating the expenses of works carried out under the Act. It corresponds to s 56 of the 1939 Act.

Section 11(1)—The presumption is that the building owner pays.

Section 11(3), (10), (11)—These sections create contingent liabilities (see para **14.10**).

Section 11(6)—This section relates also to s 7(3) (see para **6.7**).

Section 11(8)—See paras **6.9–6.10**.

Section 11(9)—The adjoining owner can 'require' works to be carried out in his counter-notice (s 4(1)(b)), and they will be within this section. He can also require underpinning under s 6(3), but that is at the expense of the building owner (see paras **5.7.1** and **11.4.5**).

Section 11(10)—The reference to 'the owner of the building' is a unique land-based description, suggesting that the reference to 'adjoining owner' here includes successors in title (see paras **5.7.2** and **14.2**).

---

12   Security for expenses

(1) An adjoining owner may serve a notice requiring the building owner before he begins any work in the exercise of the rights conferred by this Act to give such security as may be agreed between the owners or in the event of dispute determined in accordance with section 10.

(2) Where—

   (a)   in the exercise of the rights conferred by this Act an adjoining owner requires the building owner to carry out any work the expenses of which are to be defrayed in whole or in part by the adjoining owner; or
   (b)   an adjoining owner serves a notice on the building owner under subsection (1),

the building owner may before beginning the work to which the requirement or notice relates serve a notice on the adjoining owner requiring him to give such security as may be agreed between the owners or in the event of dispute determined in accordance with section 10.

(3) If within the period of one month beginning with—

   (a)   the day on which a notice is served under subsection (2); or
   (b)   in the event of dispute, the date of the determination by the surveyor or surveyors,

the adjoining owner does not comply with the notice or the determination, the requirement or notice by him to which the building owner's notice under that subsection relates shall cease to have effect.

Commentary in text—Chapter 12.

This section provides for security for costs to be available to either party. It corresponds to s 57 of the 1939 Act.

Section 12(2)(a)—See ss 4 and 11(7) and (9).

---

13   Account for work carried out

(1) Within the period of two months beginning with the day of the completion of any work executed by a building owner of which the expenses are to be wholly or partially defrayed by an adjoining owner in accordance with section 11 the building owner shall serve on the adjoining owner an account in writing showing—

   (a)   particulars and expenses of the work; and
   (b)   any deductions to which the adjoining owner or any other person is entitled in respect of old materials or otherwise;

and in preparing the account the work shall be estimated and valued at fair average rates and prices according to the nature of the work, the locality and the cost of labour and materials prevailing at the time when the work is executed.

(2) Within the period of one month beginning with the day of service of the said account the adjoining owner may serve on the building owner a notice stating any objection he may have thereto and thereupon a dispute shall be deemed to have arisen between the parties.

(3) If within that period of one month the adjoining owner does not serve notice under subsection (2) he shall be deemed to have no objection to the account.

Commentary in text—paragraph 11.7.

This section provides for the building owner to supply the adjoining owner with an account of any expenses due from him. It corresponds to s 58 of the 1939 Act.

Due delivery of the account was held to be a condition precedent to the recovery of the costs (see *Spiers and Son Ltd v Troup* (1915) 84 LJKB 1986).

---

14   Settlement of account

(1) All expenses to be defrayed by an adjoining owner in accordance with an account served under section 13 shall be paid by the adjoining owner.

(2) Until an adjoining owner pays to the building owner such expenses as aforesaid the property in any works executed under this Act to which the expenses relate shall be vested solely in the building owner.

Commentary in text—paragraphs **11.8**, **14.10** and **14.13**.

This section enables the building owner to recover contributions due from the adjoining owner. It corresponds to s 59 of the 1939 Act.

Section 14(2)—This vesting probably amounts to a statutory charge securing repayment. It appears to be a Class B land charge.

Miscellaneous

15   Service of notices etc.

(1) A notice or other document required or authorised to be served under this Act may be served on a person—

- (a)   by delivering it to him in person;
- (b)   by sending it by post to him at his usual or last-known residence or place of business in the United Kingdom; or
- (c)   in the case of a body corporate, by delivering it to the secretary or clerk of the body corporate at its registered or principal office or sending it by post to the secretary or clerk of that body corporate at that office.

(2) In the case of a notice or other document required or authorised to be served under this Act on a person as owner of premises, it may alternatively be served by—

- (a)   addressing it 'the owner' of the premises (naming them), and
- (b)   delivering it to a person on the premises or, if no person to whom it can be delivered is found there, fixing it to a conspicuous part of the premises.

Commentary in text—Chapter 13.

Where there are joint building owners, notices must be served by or on behalf of all of them (see *Lehmann v Herman* [1993] 1 EGLR 172), but where there are joint adjoining owners, service on one has been held to suffice (see *Crosby v Alhambra Co Ltd* [1907] 1 Ch 295).

---

16   Offences

(1) If—

- (a)   an occupier of land or premises refuses to permit a person to do anything which he is entitled to do with regard to the land or premises under section 8(1) or (5); and
- (b)   the occupier knows or has reasonable cause to believe that the person is so entitled,

the occupier is guilty of an offence.

(2) If—

    (a)   a person hinders or obstructs a person in attempting to do anything which he is entitled to do with regard to land or premises under section 8(1) or (5); and

    (b)   the first-mentioned person knows or has reasonable cause to believe that the other person is so entitled,

the first-mentioned person is guilty of an offence.

(3) A person guilty of an offence under subsection (1) or (2) is liable on summary conviction to a fine of an amount not exceeding level 3 on the standard scale.

Commentary in text—Chapter 16.

This section creates new criminal offences by occupiers and others. It corresponds to s 148 of the 1939 Act.

---

17 Recovery of sums

Any sum payable in pursuance of this Act (otherwise than by way of fine) shall be recoverable summarily as a civil debt.

Commentary in text—paragraph **9.5**.

This section provides a summary civil remedy for the recovery of moneys. It corresponds to s 59(1) of the 1939 Act.

---

18 Exception in case of Temples etc.

(1) This Act shall not apply to land which is situated in inner London and in which there is an interest belonging to—

    (a)   the Honourable Society of the Inner Temple,
    (b)   the Honourable Society of the Middle Temple,
    (c)   the Honourable Society of Lincoln's Inn, or
    (d)   the Honourable Society of Gray's Inn.

(2) The reference in subsection (1) to inner London is to Greater London other than the outer London boroughs.

This section exempts certain land of the Inns of Court. It corresponds to s 152 of the 1939 Act. See paragraph **1.6**.

---

19 The Crown

(1) This Act shall apply to land in which there is—

    (a)   an interest belonging to Her Majesty in right of the Crown,

(b)   an interest belonging to a government department, or

(c)   an interest held in trust for Her Majesty for the purposes of any such department.

(2) This Act shall apply to—

(a)   land which is vested in, but not occupied by, Her Majesty in right of the Duchy of Lancaster;

(b)   land which is vested in, but not occupied by, the possessor for the time being of the Duchy of Cornwall.

This section deals with application to the Crown. It corresponds to s 151 of the 1939 Act. See paragraph **1.6**.

---

20   Interpretation

In this Act, unless the context otherwise requires, the following expressions have the meanings hereby respectively assigned to them—

'adjoining owner' and 'adjoining occupier' respectively mean any owner and any occupier of land, buildings, storeys or rooms adjoining those of the building owner and for the purposes only of section 6 within the distances specified in that section;

'appointing officer' means the person appointed under this Act by the local authority to make such appointments as are required under section 10(8);

'building owner' means an owner of land who is desirous of exercising rights under this Act;

'foundation', in relation to a wall, means the solid ground or artificially formed support resting on solid ground on which the wall rests;

'owner' includes—

(a)   a person in receipt of, or entitled to receive, the whole or part of the rents or profits of land;

(b)   a person in possession of land, otherwise than as a mortgagee or as a tenant from year to year or for a lesser term or as a tenant at will;

(c)   a purchaser of an interest in land under a contract for purchase or under an agreement for a lease, otherwise than under an agreement for a tenancy from year to year or for a lesser term;

'party fence wall' means a wall (not being part of a building) which stands on lands of different owners and is used or constructed to be used for separating such adjoining lands, but does not include a wall constructed on the land of one owner the artificially formed support of which projects into the land of another owner;

'party structure' means a party wall and also a floor partition or other structure separating buildings or parts of buildings approached solely by separate staircases or separate entrances;

'party wall' means—

(a)   a wall which forms part of a building and stands on lands of different owners to a greater extent than the projection of any artificially formed support on which the wall rests; and

(b)   so much of a wall not being a wall referred to in paragraph (a) above as separates buildings belonging to different owners;

'special foundations' means foundations in which an assemblage of beams or rods is employed for the purpose of distributing any load; and

'surveyor' means any person not being a party to the matter appointed or selected under section 10 to determine disputes in accordance with the procedures set out in this Act.

Commentary in text—paragraphs **2.2–2.5**.

'Adjoining owner'—the reference to s 6 is new. The reference to s 6 suggests the strict meaning of 'adjoining'.

'Building owner'—is new.

'Owner'—paragraph (c) is new.

'Party structure'—The words 'from without' have been dropped.

'Special foundations'—The word 'steel' before 'beams' has been dropped.

---

21   Other statutory provisions

(1) The Secretary of State may by order amend or repeal any provision of a private or local Act passed before or in the same session as this Act, if it appears to him necessary or expedient to do so in consequence of this Act.

(2) An order under subsection (1) may—

(a)   contain such savings or transitional provisions as the Secretary of State thinks fit;

(b)   make different provision for different purposes.

(3) The power to make an order under subsection (1) shall be exercisable by statutory instrument subject to annulment in pursuance of a resolution of either House of Parliament.

It is expected that Part VI of the 1939 Act will be repealed under s 21(1) when the Act is brought into force. See paragraph **1.7**.

General

22   Short title, commencement and extent

(1) This Act may be cited as the Party Wall etc. Act 1996.

(2) This Act shall come into force in accordance with provision made by the Secretary of State by order made by statutory instrument.

(3) An order under subsection (2) may—

(a) contain such savings or transitional provisions as the Secretary of State thinks fit;

(b) make different provision for different purposes.

(4) This Act extends to England and Wales only.

The Act is expected to be brought fully into force on 1 April 1997. See paragraph **1.7**.

Appendix 2

The Party Walls etc Act 1996 replaces Part VI (ss 44–59) of the London Building Acts (Amendment) Act 1939. The 1939 Act is set out below so that in considering the continuing relevance of cases decided under it, readers can compare the wording of its provisions with that of the corresponding provisions in the 1996 Act.

LONDON BUILDING ACTS (AMENDMENT) ACT 1939
(2 & 3 Geo 6 c xcvii)
ARRANGEMENT OF SECTIONS

PART VI

RIGHTS ETC OF BUILDING AND ADJOINING OWNERS

PART VI

RIGHTS ETC OF BUILDING AND ADJOINING OWNERS

44 Interpretation of Part VI[1]

In this Part of this Act unless the context otherwise requires the following expressions have the meanings hereby respectively assigned to them:

'foundation' in relation to a wall means the solid ground or artificially formed support resting on solid ground on which the wall rests;

'party wall' means—

(i) a wall which forms part of a building and stands on lands of different owners to a greater extent than the projection of any artificially formed support on which the wall rests; and

(ii) so much of a wall not being a wall referred to in the foregoing paragraph (i) as separates buildings belonging to different owners;

'special foundations' means foundations in which an assemblage of steel beams or rods is employed for the purpose of distributing any load.

Rights etc of owners

45 Rights of owners of adjoining lands where junction line not built on

(1) Where lands of different owners adjoin and are not built on at the line of junction or are built on at the line of junction only to the extent of a boundary wall (not being a party fence wall or the external wall of a building) and either owner is about to build on any part of the line of junction the following provisions shall have effect—

---

1 Section 4 contains the following material definitions:

'(1) In this Act save as is otherwise expressly provided therein and unless the context otherwise requires the following expressions have the meanings hereby respectively assigned to them—

'occupier' (except in Part V (Means of escape in case of fire) of this Act) does not include a lodger and the expressions "occupy" and "occupation" shall be construed accordingly;

'party fence wall' means a wall (not being part of a building) which stands on lands of different owners and is used or constructed to be used for separating such adjoining lands but does not include a wall constructed on the land of one owner the artificially formed support of which projects into the land of another owner;

'party structure' means a party wall and also a floor partition or other structure separating buildings or parts of buildings approached solely by separate staircases or separate entrances from without;

'party wall' (except in Part VI (Rights etc of building and adjoining owners) of this Act) means so much of a wall which forms part of a building as is used or constructed to be used for separating adjoining buildings belonging to different owners or occupied or constructed or adapted to be occupied by different persons together with the remainder (if any) of the wall vertically above such before-mentioned portion of the wall.'

(a)   If the building owner desires to build on the line of junction a party wall or party fence wall—

　　(i)   the building owner shall serve notice of his desire on the adjoining owner describing the intended wall;

　　(ii)   if the adjoining owner consents in writing to the building of a party wall or party fence wall the wall shall be built half on the land of each of the two owners or in such other position as may be agreed between the two owners and the expense of building the wall shall be from time to time defrayed by the two owners in due proportion regard being had to the use made or to be made of the wall by the two owners respectively and to the cost of labour and materials prevailing at the time when that use is made by each owner respectively;

　　(iii)   if the adjoining owner does not consent in writing to the building of a party wall or party fence wall the building owner shall not build the wall otherwise than at his own expense and as an external wall or a fence wall as the case may be placed wholly on his own land;

(b)   If the building owner desires to build on the line of junction a wall placed wholly on his own land he shall serve notice of his desire on the adjoining owner describing the intended wall;

(c)   Where in either of the cases described in paragraphs (a) and (b) of this subsection the building owner builds a wall on his own land he shall have a right at his own expense at any time after the expiration of one month but not exceeding six months from the service of the notice to place on land of the adjoining owner below the level of such land any projecting footings and foundation making compensation to the adjoining owner or the adjoining occupier or both of them for any damage occasioned thereby the amount of the compensation in the event of difference to be determined in the manner provided in this Part of this Act.

(2) Nothing in this section shall authorise the building owner to place special foundations on land of the adjoining owner without his previous consent in writing.

46   Rights of owners of adjoining lands where junction line built on

(1) Where lands of different owners adjoin and at the line of junction the said lands are built on or a boundary wall being a party fence wall or the external wall of a building has been erected the building owner shall have the following rights—

(a)   A right to make good underpin thicken or repair or demolish and rebuild a party structure or party fence wall in any case where such work is necessary on account of defect or want of repair of the party structure or party fence wall;

(b) A right to demolish a timber or other partition which separates buildings belonging to different owners but is not in conformity with the London Building Acts or the Building Regulations 1985 and to build instead a party wall in conformity with those regulations;

(c) A right in relation to a building having rooms or storeys belonging to different owners intermixed to demolish such of those rooms or storeys or any part thereof as are not in conformity with the London Building Acts or the Building Regulations 1985 and to rebuild them in conformity with those regulations;

(d) A right (where buildings are connected by arches or structures over public ways or over passages belonging to other persons) to demolish such of those buildings arches or structures or such parts thereto as are not in conformity with the London Building Acts or the Building Regulations 1985 and to rebuild them in conformity with those regulations;

(e) A right to underpin thicken or raise any party structure or party fence wall permitted by this Act to be underpinned thickened or raised or any external wall built against such a party structure or party fence wall subject to—

    (i) making good all damage occasioned thereby to the adjoining premises or to the internal finishings and decorations thereof; and

    (ii) carrying up to such height and in such materials as may be agreed between the building owner and the adjoining owner or in the event of difference determined in the manner provided in this Part of this Act all flues and chimney stacks belonging to the adjoining owner on or against the party structure or external wall;

(f) A right to demolish a party structure which is of insufficient strength or height for the purposes of any intended building of the building owner and to rebuild it of sufficient strength or height for the said purposes subject to—

    (i) making good all damage occasioned thereby to the adjoining premises or to the internal finishings and decorations thereof; and

    (ii) carrying up to such height and in such materials as may be agreed between the building owner and the adjoining owner or in the event of difference determined in the manner provided in this Part of this Act all flues and chimney stacks belonging to the adjoining owner on or against the party structure or external wall;

(g) A right to cut into a party structure subject to making good all damage occasioned thereby to the adjoining premises or to the internal finishings and decorations thereof;

(h) A right to cut away any footing or any projecting chimney breast jamb or flue or other projection on or over the land of the building owner from a party wall party fence wall external wall or boundary wall in order to erect raise or underpin an external wall against such party wall party fence wall external wall or boundary wall or for any other purpose subject to making good all damage occasioned thereby to the adjoining premises or to the internal finishings and decorations thereof;

(i) A right to cut away or demolish such parts of any wall or building of an adjoining owner overhanging the land of the building owner as may be necessary to enable a vertical wall to be erected against that wall or building subject to making good any damage occasioned thereby to the wall or building or to the internal finishings and decorations of the adjoining premises;

(j) A right to execute any other necessary works incidental to the connection of a party structure with the premises adjoining it;

(k) A right to raise a party fence wall to raise and use as a party wall a party fence wall or to demolish a party fence wall and rebuild it as a party fence wall or as a party wall.

(2) For the purposes of this section a . . . structure which was erected before the 6th January 1986 shall be deemed to be in conformity with the London Building Acts and a building which was erected before that date shall be deemed to be in conformity with those Acts and the Building Regulations 1985 if it is in conformity with the Acts and any byelaws made in pursuance of the Acts which regulated buildings or structures in London at the date at which it was erected.

(3) Nothing in this section shall authorise the building owner to place special foundations on land of the adjoining owner without his previous consent in writing.

47 Party structure notices

(1) Before exercising any right conferred on him by section 46 (Rights of owners of adjoining lands where junction line built on) of this Act a building owner shall serve on the adjoining owner notice in writing (in this Act referred to as a 'party structure notice') stating the nature and particulars of the proposed work the time at which it will be begun and those particulars shall where the building owner proposes to construct special foundations include plans sections and details of construction of the special foundations with reasonable particulars of the loads to be carried thereby.

(2) A party structure notice shall be served—
  (a) in respect of a party fence wall or special foundations at least one month; and
  (b) in respect of a party structure at least two months;

before the date stated therein as that on which the work is to be begun.

(3) A party structure notice shall not be effective unless the work to which the notice relates is begun within six months after the notice has been served and is prosecuted with due diligence.

(4) Nothing in this section shall prevent a building owner from exercising with the consent in writing of the adjoining owner and of the adjoining occupiers any right conferred on him by section 46 (Rights of owners of adjoining lands where junction line built on) of this Act and nothing in this section shall require him to serve any party structure notice before complying with any notice served under the provisions of Part VII (Dangerous and neglected structures) of this Act.

48   Counter notices

(1) After the service of a party structure notice the adjoining owner may serve on the building owner a notice in writing (in this Part of this Act referred to as 'a counter notice').

(2) A counter notice—

(a)   may in respect of a party fence wall or party structure require the building owner to build in or on the party fence wall or party structure as the case may be to which the notice relates such chimney copings breasts jambs or flues or such piers or recesses or other like works as may reasonably be required for the convenience of the adjoining owner;

(b)   may in respect of special foundations to which the adjoining owner consents under subsection (3) of section 46 (Rights of owners of adjoining lands where junction line built on) of this Act require them to be placed at a specified greater depth than that proposed by the building owner or to be constructed of sufficient strength to bear the load to be carried by columns of any intended building of the adjoining owner or may include both of these requirements; and

(c)   shall specify the works required by the notice to be executed and shall be accompanied by plans sections and particulars thereof.

(3) A counter notice shall be served—

(a)   in relation to special foundations within twenty-one days after the service of the party structure notice; and

(b)   in relation to any other matter within one month after the service of the party structure notice.

(4) A building owner on whom a counter notice has been served shall comply with the requirements of the counter notice unless the execution of the works required by the counter notice would be injurious to him or cause unnecessary inconvenience to him or unnecessary delay in the execution of the works pursuant to the party structure notice.

49   Dissent from notices

If an owner on whom a party structure notice or a counter notice has been served does not within fourteen days thereafter express his consent thereto in writing he shall be deemed to have dissented from the notice and a difference shall be deemed to have arisen between the parties.

50 Underpinning
(1) Where a building owner—

(a) proposes to erect within ten feet from any part of a building of an adjoining owner a building or structure independent of the building of the adjoining owner and any part of the proposed building or structure will within the said ten feet extend to a lower level than the level of the bottom of the foundations of the building of the adjoining owner; or

(b) proposes to erect within twenty feet from any part of an independent building of an adjoining owner a building or structure any part of which will within the said twenty feet meet a plane drawn downwards in the direction of the building or structure of the building owner at an angle of forty-five degrees to the horizontal from the line formed by the intersection of the plane of the level of the bottom of the foundations of the building of the adjoining owner with the plane of the external face of the external wall of the building of the adjoining owner;

he may and if required by the adjoining owner shall subject to the provisions of this section at the expense of the building owner underpin or otherwise strengthen or safeguard the foundations of the building of the adjoining owner so far as may be necessary.

(2) In any case to which subsection (1) of this section applies the following provisions shall have effect—

(a) At least one month before beginning to erect a building or structure the building owner shall serve on the adjoining owner notice in writing of his intention so to do and that notice shall state whether he proposes to underpin or otherwise strengthen or safeguard the foundations of the building of the adjoining owner;

(b) The said notice shall be accompanied by plans and sections showing the site of the building or structure proposed to be erected by the building owner and the depth to which he proposes to excavate;

(c) Within fourteen days after service of the said notice the adjoining owner may serve notice in writing on the building that he disputes the necessity of or requires as the case may be the underpinning or strengthening or the safeguarding of the foundations of his building and if the adjoining owner serves such a notice a difference shall be deemed to have arisen between the building owner and the adjoining owner;

(d) The building owner shall compensate the adjoining owner and any adjoining occupier for any inconvenience loss or damage which may result to any of them by reason of any work executed in pursuance of this section.

(3) On completion of any work executed in pursuance of this section the building owner shall if so requested by the adjoining owner supply him with particulars including plans and sections of the work.

(4) Nothing in this section shall relieve the building owner from any liability to which he would otherwise be subject for injury to the adjoining owner or any adjoining occupier by reason of work executed by him.

51 Execution of works

(1) A building owner shall not exercise any right conferred on him by this Part of this Act in such manner or at such time as to cause unnecessary inconvenience to the adjoining owner or to the adjoining occupier.

(2) Where a building owner in exercising any right conferred on him by this Part of this Act lays open any part of the adjoining land or building he shall at his own expense make and maintain so long as may be necessary a proper hoarding shoring or fans or temporary construction for the protection of the adjoining land or building and the security of the adjoining occupier.

(3) Any works executed in pursuance of this Part of this Act shall—

(a) comply with the provisions of the London Building Acts and the Building Regulations 1985; and
(b) subject to the foregoing paragraph (a) be executed in accordance with such plans sections and particulars as may be agreed between the owners or in the event of difference determined in the manner provided in this Part of this Act and no deviation shall be made therefrom except such as may also be agreed between the parties or in the event of difference determined in manner aforesaid.

52 Notice of excavation of sites abutting on narrow streets or ways

Where a building owner proposes to erect any building or structure or carry out any work in relation to a building or structure on land which abuts on a street or way less than twenty feet in width the following provisions shall have effect if the erection of the proposed building or structure or the carrying out of the work involves excavation to a depth of twenty feet or more below the level of the highest part of the land immediately abutting on the street—

(a) Notices stating the place (being a place situate at a distance not greater than two miles of such land) at and the hours during which plans and sections of so much of the proposed building structure or work as relates to the excavation may be inspected shall be exhibited in a prominent position on the land or on any existing building or on the boundary wall fence or hoarding (if any) surrounding the said land or building and in such a manner as to be readily legible from every street or way on which the land abuts;
(b) The notices shall be exhibited at least four weeks before any such work of excavation is begun and shall be maintained and where necessary renewed by the building owner until such work of excavation is begun;
(c) The plans and sections referred to in the notices shall until the work of excavation is begun be open to public inspection without payment at the place and during such reasonable hours as are stated in the notice.

53 Power of entry by building owner

(1) A building owner his servants agents and workmen may during usual working hours enter and remain on any premises for the purpose of executing and may execute any work in pursuance of this Part of this Act and may remove any furniture or fittings or take any other action necessary for that purpose.

(2) If the premises are closed the building owner his servants agents and workmen may if accompanied by a constable or other police officer break open any fences or doors in order to enter the premises.

(3) Before entering any premises in pursuance of this section a building owner shall give to the owner and occupier of the premises—

- (a) in case of emergency such notice of his intention to enter as may be reasonably practicable;
- (b) in any other case fourteen days' notice of his intention to enter.

54 Saving for easements

Nothing in this Part shall authorise any interference with any easement of light or other easement in or relating to a party wall or prejudicially affect the right of any person to preserve any right in connection with a party wall which is demolished or rebuilt and to take any necessary steps for that purpose.

Differences between owners

55 Settlement of differences

Where a difference arises or is deemed to have arisen between a building owner and an adjoining owner in respect of any matter connected with any work to which this Part of this Act relates the following provisions shall have effect:

- (a) Either—

  - (i) both parties shall concur in the appointment of one surveyor (in this section referred to as an 'agreed surveyor'); or
  - (ii) each party shall appoint a surveyor and the two surveyors so appointed shall select a third surveyor (all of whom are in this section together referred to as 'the three surveyors');

- (b) If an agreed surveyor refuses or for ten days after a written request by either party neglects to act or if before the difference is settled he dies or becomes incapable of acting the proceedings for settling such difference shall begin de novo;
- (c) If either party to the difference refuses or for ten days after a written request by the other party neglects to appoint a surveyor under subparagraph (ii) of paragraph (a) of this section that other party may make the appointment on his behalf;
- (d) If before the difference is settled a surveyor appointed under subparagraph (ii) of paragraph (a) of this section by a party to the difference dies or becomes incapable of acting the party who appointed him may

appoint another surveyor in his place who shall have the same power and authority as his predecessor;

(e) If a surveyor appointed under subparagraph (ii) of paragraph (a) of this section by a party to the difference or if a surveyor appointed under paragraph (d) of this section refuses or for ten days after a written request by either party neglects to act the surveyor of the other party may proceed ex parte and anything so done by him shall be as effectual as if he had been an agreed surveyor;

(f) If a surveyor appointed under subparagraph (ii) of paragraph (a) of this section by a party to the difference refuses or for ten days after a written request by either party neglects to select a third surveyor under paragraph (a) or paragraph (g) of this section the superintending architect or in cases where the Council is a party to the difference the Secretary of State may on the application of either party select a third surveyor who shall have the same power and authority as if he had been selected under paragraph (a) or paragraph (g) of this section;

(g) If a third surveyor selected under subparagraph (ii) of paragraph (a) of this section refuses or for ten days after a written request by either party or the surveyor appointed by either party neglects to act or if before the difference is settled he dies or becomes incapable of acting the other two of the three surveyors shall forthwith select another surveyor in his place who shall have the same power and authority as his precedessor;

(h) All appointments and selections made under this section shall be in writing;

(i) The agreed surveyor or as the case may be the three surveyors or any two of them shall settle by award any matter which before the commencement of any work to which a notice under this Part of this Act relates or from time to time during the continuance of such work may be in dispute between the building owner and the adjoining owner;

(j) If no two of the three surveyors are in agreement the third surveyor selected in pursuance of this section shall make the award within fourteen days after he is called upon to do so;

(k) The award may determine the right to execute and the time and manner of executing any work and generally any other matter arising out of or incidental to the difference:

Provided that any period appointed by the award for executing any work shall not unless otherwise agreed between the building owner and the adjoining owner begin to run until after the expiration of the period prescribed by this Act for service of the notice in respect of which the difference arises or is deemed to have arisen;

(l) The costs incurred in making or obtaining an award under this section and the cost of reasonable supervision of carrying out any work to which the award relates shall subject to the provisions of this section be paid by such of the parties as the surveyor or surveyors making the award determine;

(m) The award shall be conclusive and shall not except as provided by this section be questioned in any court;

(n) Either of the parties to the difference may within fourteen days after the delivery of an award made under this section appeal to the county court against the award and the following provisions shall have effect—

    (i) Subject as hereafter in this paragraph provided the county court may rescind the award or modify it in such manner and make such order as to costs as it thinks fit;

    (ii) If the appellant against the award on appearing before the county court is unwilling that the matter should be decided by that court and satisfies that court that he will if the matter is decided against him be liable to pay a sum (exclusive of costs) exceeding one hundred pounds and gives security approved by the county court to prosecute his appeal in the High Court and to abide the event thereof all proceedings in the county court shall be stayed and the appellant may bring an action in the High Court against the other party to the difference;

(o) Where an appellant against an award brings an action in the High Court in pursuance of the last preceding paragraph the following provisions shall have effect—

    (i) If the parties agree as to the facts a special case may be stated for the opinion of the court and may be dealt with in accordance with or as nearly as circumstances admit in accordance with the rules of the court;

    (ii) In any other case the plaintiff in the action shall deliver to the defendant an issue whereby the matters in difference may be tried;

    (iii) The issue shall be in such form as may be agreed between the parties or in case of dispute or of non-appearance of the defendant as may be settled by the court;

    (iv) The action shall proceed and the issue be tried in accordance with or as nearly as circumstances admit in accordance with the rules of the court;

    (v) Any costs incurred by the parties in the county courts shall be deemed to be costs incurred in the action in the High Court and be payable accordingly.

Expenses

56 Expenses in respect of party structures

(1) The following provisions shall apply with respect to the apportionment of expenses as between the building owner and the adjoining owner—

(a) Expenses incurred in the exercise of the rights conferred by paragraph (a) of subsection (1) of section 46 (Rights of owners of adjoining lands where junction line built on) of this Act shall be defrayed by the building owner and the adjoining owner in due proportion regard being had to the use which the two owners respectively make or may make of the party structure or party fence wall;

(b) Expenses incurred in the exercise of the rights conferred by paragraph (b) of subsection (1) of the said section together with the expenses of building any additional party structure that may be required by reason of the exercise of those rights shall be defrayed by the building owner and the adjoining owner in due proportion regard being had to the use which the two owners respectively make or may make of the party wall or party structure and the thickness of such party wall or party structure required for support of the respective buildings of the two owners;

(c) Expenses incurred in the exercise of the rights conferred by paragraph (c) of subsection (1) of the said section shall be defrayed by the building owner and the adjoining owner in due proportion regard being had to the use which the two owners respectively make or may make of the rooms or storeys rebuilt;

(d) Expenses incurred in the exercise of the rights conferred by paragraph (d) of subsection (1) of the said section shall be defrayed by the building owner and the adjoining owner in due proportion regard being had to the use which the two owners respectively make or may make of the buildings arches or structures rebuilt;

(e) Expenses incurred in the exercise of the rights conferred by—

(i) paragraphs (e) (g) (h) (i) and (k) of subsection (1) of the said section;

(ii) paragraphs (f) of subsection (1) of the said section in so far as the expenses are not expenses incurred in the exercise of any rights conferred by other paragraphs of the said subsection and also a fair allowance in respect of the disturbance and inconvenience caused where the expenses have been incurred in the exercise of the rights conferred by the said paragraph (f);

shall be defrayed by the building owner.

(2) Expenses incurred in the exercise of the rights conferred by paragraph (j) of subsection (1) of the said section shall be defrayed in the same manner as the expenses of the work to which they are incidental.

(3) Any expenses reasonably incurred by the building owner in executing any works in pursuance of a counter notice served on him by an adjoining owner under section 48 (Counter notices) of this Act shall be defrayed by the adjoining owner.

(4) If at any time during the execution or after the completion of works carried out in the exercise of the rights conferred by paragraphs (e) (f) (j) or (k) of subsection (1) of section 46 (Rights of owners of adjoining lands where junction line built on) of this Act any use of those works or any part thereof is made by the adjoining owner additional to the use thereof made by him at the time when the works began a due proportion of the expenses incurred by the

building owner in the exercise of the rights conferred by any of the said paragraphs regard being had to the additional use of the works made by the adjoining owner shall be defrayed by the adjoining owner.

(5) Where in pursuance of section 45 (Rights of owners of adjoining lands where junction line not built on) or the said section 46 of this Act consent in writing has been given to the construction of special foundations on land of an adjoining owner then if the adjoining owner erects any building or structure and its cost is found to be increased by reason of the existence of the said foundations the owner of the building to which the said foundations belong shall on receiving an account with any necessary vouchers within two months after the completion of the work by the adjoining owner repay to the adjoining owner so much of the cost as is due to the existence of the said foundations.

(6) Where under this section expenses are to be defrayed in due proportion regard being had to the use made by an owner of a party structure party fence wall external wall or other work regard shall unless otherwise agreed between the building owner and the adjoining owner or provided in the award also be had to the cost of labour and materials prevailing at the time when that use is made.

57   Security for expenses
(1) An adjoining owner may by notice in writing require the building owner before he begins any work in the exercise of the rights conferred by this Part of this Act to give such security as may be agreed between the owners or in the event of dispute determined by a judge of the county court for the payment of all such expenses costs and compensation in respect of the work as may be payable by the building owner.

(2) Where in the exercise of the rights conferred by this Part of this Act an adjoining owner requires a building owner to carry out any work the expenses of which are to be defrayed in whole or in part by the adjoining owner or where the adjoining owner serves a notice on the building owner under subsection (1) of this section the building owner may before beginning the work to which the requirement or notice relates serve a notice in writing on the adjoining owner requiring him to give such security as may be agreed between the owners or in the event of dispute determined by a judge of the county court for the payment of such expenses costs and compensation in respect of the work as may be payable by him.

(3) If within one month after receiving a notice under subsection (2) of this section or in the event of dispute after the date of the determination by the judge of the county court the adjoining owner does not comply therewith the requirement or notice by him to which the building owner's notice under that subsection relates shall cease to have effect.

58   Account of expenses
(1) Within two months after the completion of any work executed by a building owner of which the expenses are to be wholly or partially defrayed by an

adjoining owner in accordance with section 56 (Expenses in respect of party structures) of this Act the building owner shall deliver to the adjoining owner an account in writing showing—

    (a) particulars and expenses of the work; and

    (b) any deductions to which the adjoining owner or any other person is entitled in respect of old materials or otherwise;

and in preparing the account the work shall be estimated and valued at fair average rates and prices according to the nature of the work the locality and the cost of labour and materials prevailing at the time when the work is executed.

(2) Within one month after delivery of the said account the adjoining owner may give notice in writing to the building owner stating any objection he may have thereto and thereupon a difference shall be deemed to have arisen between the parties.

(3) If within the said month the adjoining owner does not give notice under subsection (2) of this section he shall be deemed to have no objection to the account.

59   Recovery of expenses

(1) All expenses to be defrayed by an adjoining owner in accordance with an account delivered under section 58 (Account of expenses) of this Act shall be paid by the adjoining owner and in default may be recovered as a debt.

(2) Until an adjoining owner pays to the building owner such expenses as aforesaid the property in any works executed under this Part of this Act to which the expenses relate shall be vested solely in the building owner.

Appendix 3

CHECKLISTS OF NOTICES

1. By Building Owner on Adjoining Owner

Building Owner's Objective	Form of Notice Required	Time-Limit for Service	Authority
To build a party wall or party fence wall on the line of junction	Line of Junction Notice: *see* Precedent 1.1	At least one month before building owner intends work to start.	s 1(2)
To build on the line of junction a wall placed wholly on his own land.	Line of Junction Notice: *see* Precedent 1.2	At least one month before the building owner intends the building work to start.	s 1(5)
To carry out works to an existing party wall, party fence wall or party structure.	Party structure notice: *see* Precedent 2.	At least 2 months before the date on which the proposed work will begin.	s 3
To consent to a counter-notice	Consent Notice: *see* Precedent 5.2.	14 days beginning with the date on which the counter-notice is served.	s 5
To excavate within a distance of three metres/six metres of any part of a building or structure of an adjoining owner. **NB**: The proposed excavation must fall within s 6(1) and (2).	Three/Six-metre Notice: *see* Precedent 4.	At least one month before beginning to excavate.	s 6(5)
To require security for expenses.	Notice Requiring Security: *see* Precedent 12.2	Before beginning the work to which the requirement or notice relates. Security must be given by adjoining owner within one month of notice or determination by surveyor(s)	s 12(2)
To recover from adjoining owner expenses to be wholly or partly defrayed by adjoining owner.	Account: *see* Precedent 14.	Two months from completion of the work.	s 13(1)

2. By Building Owner on Adjoining Occupiers as well as Adjoining Owners

Building Owner's Objective	Form of Notice Required	Time-Limit for Service	Authority
To exercise rights of entry in order to execute works under the Act.	Notice of Entry: *see* Precedent 7.1	*Normally*: not less than 14 days before the proposed entry. *In emergencies*: such period as may be reasonably practicable.	s 8(3)
To enable a surveyor appointed or selected under s 10 to enter land or premises during usual working hours for the purpose of carrying out the object for which he is appointed or selected.	Notice of Entry: *see* Precedent 7.2	*Normally*: not less than 14 days before the day of the proposed entry. *In emergencies*: such period as may be reasonably practicable.	s 8(6)

3. By Adjoining Owner on Building Owner

Adjoining Owner's Objective	Form of Notice Required	Time-Limit for Service	Authority
To consent to the building of a party wall or a party fence wall. For the consequences see para **3.3.2.**	Consent Notice: *see* Precedent 5.1.	No time specified.	s 1(3)
To consent to the building of a party wall or party fence wall.	Consent Notice: *see* Precedent 5.1.	14 days beginning with the date on which the notice under section 1(2) is served.	s 1(4)
To consent to party structure notice.	Consent Notice: *see* Precedent 5.1	14 days beginning with the date on which the party structure notice is served.	s 5
To consent to party structure notice subject to requiring works as specified in s 4(1).	Counter-notice: *see* Precedent 3.	One month beginning with the date on which the party structure notice is served.	s 4(1)
To require building owner to maintain existing height of the wall.	Counter-notice under s 4(1) (*see* above).	(as above)	s 11(7)

3. By Adjoining Owner on Building Owner

Adjoining Owner's Objective	Form of Notice Required	Time-Limit for Service	Authority
To consent to notice by building owner under s 6(5).	Consent Notice: *see* Precedent 5.1.	14 days beginning with service of notice under section 6(5).	s 6(7)
To recover his extra cost of building on his land incurred by reason of the existence of special foundations.	Account justifying claim: any necessary invoices and other supporting documents must be supplied.	No time specified. Building owner must pay account within 2 months.	s 11(10)
To require security for expenses.	Notice Requiring Security: *see* Precedent 12.1.	Before work begins.	s 12(1)
To object to account served by building owner. Details of objection to be given.	Notice of Objections to Account: *see* Precedent 15.	One month after service of the account.	s 13(2)

Appendix 4

PRECEDENTS

1. Line of Junction Notice[1]

Party Wall etc Act 1996 ('the 1996 Act')

To: [Name of Adjoining Owner]
of   [Address]

From: [Name of Building Owner]
of   [Address]

THIS is a notice under section 1(2) [1(5)] of the 1996 Act relating to the boundary between my property at   and your adjoining property at

1. I HEREBY GIVE YOU NOTICE as follows:

1.1   [If the notice is under section 1(2)]
     (a) I desire to build a party [fence] wall on the line of junction between our said properties.
     (b) If you agree to this work I request that you serve on me a notice indicating your consent within 14 days of this notice being served on you. This will lead to the consequences set out in section 1(3) of the 1996 Act.
     (c) If you do not serve such a notice, I shall be entitled to carry out the work at my own expense, wholly on my own property (apart from the footings and foundations mentioned below)

1.2   [If the notice is under section 1(5)]
I desire to build along the line of junction between our said properties a wall which will be placed wholly on my own property, apart from the footings and foundations mentioned below.

2.   (a) The work involved is described in the attached plans [specifications and drawings].[2]
     (b) The work includes the placing of projecting footings and foundations below the level of your property, which I have a right to do under section 1(6) of the 1996 Act.[3]

3.   I propose to start work after the expiration of one month from the date this notice is served on you, or earlier if you agree.[4]

4.   If a dispute arises between us over this work, it has to be referred to one or more Surveyors under section 10 of the 1996 Act. For the purposes of any dispute I appoint Mr   of   as my Surveyor, and invite you to concur in appointing him as an agreed Surveyor.[5]

Signed [by the Building Owner or authorised agent]

Dated:

Notes

1 This Precedent incorporates notices under both s 1(2) and (5).

2 Section 1 does not require plans, but they are sure to be advisable.

3 Projecting footings and foundations are likely (or s 1 may not apply). If special foundations are required, incorporate cl 1(c) from Precedent 2.

4 At least one month's notice is required by both sections.

5 Clause 4 is not essential, but may expedite the appointment of surveyors (for the agreed surveyor see s 10(1)(a)).

2.   Party Structure Notice[1]

Party Wall etc Act 1996 ('the 1996 Act')

To: [Name of Adjoining Owner]
of   [Address]

From: [Name of Building Owner]
of   [Address]

THIS is a Party Structure Notice under section 3 of the 1996 Act relating to the structure on the boundary between my property at

and your adjoining property at

I HEREBY GIVE YOU NOTICE as follows:
1.   (a) I propose to carry out works to or upon the said structure in exercise of my rights under section 2(2) of the 1996 Act [and in particular sub-sections (a), (b), (c), etc.[2]]
        (b) The nature and particulars of the proposed works are fully described in the attached plans, specifications and drawings ('the Plans').
        (c) The proposed works [do not] include special foundations [and the Plans include full details of them and the loads to be carried by them. I am not entitled to construct special foundations in your land without your written consent].[3]

2.   I propose to begin work after the expiration of two months from the date this notice is served on you, or earlier if you agree.[4]

3.   (a) If you agree to the works, I request that you serve on me a notice indicating your consent within 14 days of this notice being served on you.
        (b) If you wish to propose modifications to the works, you may be entitled to serve a counter-notice under section 4 of the 1996 Act within one month of this notice being served on you.
        (c) If you do not act under (a) or (b) a dispute is deemed to arise between us, which has to be referred to one or more Surveyors under section 10 of the 1996 Act.[5]

4.   For the purposes of any dispute I appoint Mr   of
        as my Surveyor, and invite you to concur in appointing him as an agreed Surveyor.[6]

Signed [by Building Owner or authorised agent]

Dated:

Notes

1 See s 3. This notice is the essential preliminary to exercising rights under s 2, which applies when the boundary is already built on.
2 It is desirable to specify as accurately and completely as possible the subsections under which the works will be carried out.
3 Clauses 1 and 2 are required by s 3(1).
4 At least 2 months' notice of starting work is required (s 3(2)(a)).
5 Clause 3 is not essential, but helps to explain clause 4.
6 Clause 4 is not essential, but could expedite the appointment of surveyors (for the agreed Surveyor see s 10(1)(a)).

3.   Counter-notice to Party Structure Notice[1]

Party Wall etc Act 1996 ('the 1996 Act')

To: [Name of Building Owner]
of   [Address]
From: [Name of Adjoining Owner]
of   [Address]

This is a Counter-notice under section 4(1) of the 1996 Act in response to the notice dated   and served by you on me under section 3 of the 1996 Act.

I HEREBY GIVE YOU NOTICE as follows:

1.   I require:
    (a) that you build in or on the structure to which your notice relates chimney copings [breasts / jambs / flues / piers / recesses / other works] as specified in the attached plans, specifications and particulars ('the Plans'), which are works reasonably required for my convenience;[2]
    (b) that the special foundations referred to in your notice
       (i) be placed at the depth specified in the Plans, and
      (iii) be constructed of the strength specified in the Plans, which is designed to bear the load to be carried by columns of a building intended by me.[3]

2.   Subject to the foregoing requirements and without prejudice to any of my rights under the 1996 Act or otherwise, I consent to the works proposed in your notice.

Signed [by Adjoining Owner or authorised agent]

Dated:[4]

Notes

1 See s 4. The point of a counter-notice is to enable the adjoining owner to consent, subject to imposing conditions of the kind permitted by s 4(1). If he wishes to dispute the party structure notice in principle, he should serve no notice, and allow a deemed dispute to arise under s 5.

2 See s 4(1)(a). The plans etc are required by s 4(2)(a).

3 See s 4(1)(b).

4 This notice must be served within one month of service of the party structure notice.

4. Three/Six-metre Notice[1]

Party Wall etc Act 1996 ('the 1996 Act')

To: [Name of Adjoining Owner]
of   [Address]

From: [Name of Building Owner]
of   [Address]

THIS is a notice under section 6(5) of the 1996 Act relating to excavation works on my property at
which will be within a prescribed distance from your adjoining property at

I HEREBY GIVE YOU NOTICE as follows:

1.   [If this is a 3-metre notice (section 6(1))]
        I propose to carry out works on my property within 3 metres of the building on your property involving excavation below the level of the bottom of its foundations.
        [If this is a 6-metre notice (section 6(2)]
        I propose to carry out works on my property within 6 metres of the building on your property involving excavation within an area defined by section 6(2) of the 1996 Act.[2]

2.   (a) The proposed works, including the site and depth of the excavation and the site of the proposed building, are fully described in the attached plans and sections ('the Plans').[3]
        (b) I [do not] propose to underpin or otherwise safeguard the foundations of the building on your property [and these works are also described in the Plans].[4]

3.   I propose to start excavating after the expiration of one month from the date this notice is served on you, or earlier if you agree.[5]

4.   If you agree to the works, I request that you serve on me a notice indicating your consent within 14 days of this notice being served on you. If you do not, a dispute is deemed to arise between us, which has to be referred to one or more Surveyors under section 10 of the 1996 Act.[6]

5.   For the purposes of any dispute I appoint Mr   of
        as my Surveyor, and invite you to concur in appointing him as an agreed Surveyor.[7]

Signed [by Building Owner of authorised agent]

Dated:

Notes

1 See s 6(1) and (2).
2 These summaries are not wholly accurate. The sections must be referred to in order to determine whether they apply. See Figure 3.
3 Clause 2(a) is required by s 6(6).
4 Clause 2(b) is required by s 6(5).
5 At least one month's notice must be given (s 6(5)).
6 See s 6(7).
7 Clauses 4 and 5 are not essential, but may expedite the appointment of Surveyors (for the agreed Surveyor see s 10(1)(a)).

5.   Consent Notices

Party Wall etc Act 1996 ('the 1996 Act')

5.1   Consents by Adjoining Owner[1]

Without prejudice to any of my rights under the 1996 Act or otherwise, I [Name of Adjoining Owner] of [Address], in response to the notice under the 1996 Act dated   and served on me by [Name of Building Owner], HEREBY GIVE NOTICE that I consent to the carrying out of the works described in that notice, subject to all the provisions of the 1996 Act.

Signed: [by or on behalf of Adjoining Owner]

Dated:

5.2   Consent by Building Owner[2]

Without prejudice to any of my rights under the 1996 Act or otherwise, I [Name of Building Owner] of [Address], in response to the counter-notice under section 4 of the 1996 Act dated   and served on me by [Name of Adjoining Owner], HEREBY GIVE NOTICE that I consent to the requirements set out in that notice, subject to all the provisions of the 1996 Act.

Signed: [by or on behalf of Building Owner]

Dated:[3]

Notes

1 This is a general form of consent notice by the adjoining owner, which can be used under ss 1(3), (4), 5 or 6(7). It should be understood that consent under s 1(3) will involve the consequences set out in that section (which are not attractive to the adjoining owner), and that consent under s 5 may be exposing him to liability for certain expenses (see Chapter 11).

2 The only occasion for a consent notice by the building owner is under s 5, if he is content with the terms of a counter-notice. He will be giving up his right under s 4(3) to dispute the requirements in the counter-notice.

3 All consent notices should be served within 14 days of service of the notice to which they consent. (The absence of a time-limit under s 1(3) is best ignored.)

6. Notice of Dispute[1]

Party Wall etc Act 1996 ('the 1996 Act')

I, [Name of Adjoining Owner] of [Address] acknowledge receipt of a [purported][2] notice under the 1996 Act dated   and addressed to me by [Name of Building Owner] ['the Notice'], and in response HEREBY GIVE NOTICE as follows:

[1.   I dispute the validity of the Notice on the ground that   ][2]

2.   I do not consent to the carrying out of the works described in the Notice.

3.   Without prejudice to 1 and 2 above:
    [(a) I require the Building Owner at his own expense to underpin or otherwise strengthen or safeguard the foundations of the building on my land[3]].
    (b) For the purpose of the dispute I appoint Mr   of to be my Surveyor [concur in the appointment of Mr   of   as the agreed Surveyor].

Signed: [by or on behalf of Adjoining Owner]

Dated:

Notes

1 The Act does not require any formal notice of dispute, but this Precedent will be useful: (a) under s 1, where deemed disputes do not arise; (b) in order to attack the validity of the building owner's notice: and (c) for requiring underpinning under s 6(3).

2 Clause 1 and the word 'purported' should be included or omitted together. There are many grounds for disputing the validity of a notice (eg bad service, insufficient details of works, building owner or works not qualifying).

3 Clause 3 must not give away clauses 1 and 2. For (a) see s 6(3).

7.   Notice of Entry[1]

Party Wall etc Act 1996 ('the 1996 Act')

To: (1) The Owner of [Address of Adjoining Premises][2] ('the Premises')

(2) [Name] and [Name], the occupiers of the Premises[3]

From: [Name of Building Owner] of [Address]

THIS is a notice under section 8(3)[(6)] of the 1996 Act of intention to enter the Premises.

I HEREBY GIVE YOU NOTICE as follows:

1.   After the expiration of 14 days[4] from the date that this notice is served on you

7.1   [If the notice is under section 8(3)]

I intend to enter the Premises with my agents and workmen [and principally my contractors, Messrs.   ]
for the purpose of executing the works authorised by an Award dated   and made under the 1996 Act. For that purpose they are entitled under section 8(1) of the 1996 Act to enter and remain on the Premises during usual working hours, and to remove any furniture or fittings and take any other action necessary.

7.2   [If the notice is under section 8(6)]

The Surveyors appointed for the purposes of a dispute under the 1996 Act, namely Mr   of   and Mr   of   intend to enter the Premises for the purpose of carrying out the object for which they are appointed. For that purpose they are entitled under section 8(5) of the 1996 Act to enter and remain on the Premises during usual working hours.

2.   Under section 16 of the 1996 Act it is an offence:

   (a) for an occupier of premises to refuse to permit a person to do anything which he is entitled to do with regard to the premises under section 8(1) or (5) of the 1996 Act, if the occupier knows or has reasonable cause to believe he is so entitled;
   (b) for any person to hinder or obstruct another in attempting to do anything which he is so entitled to do with regard to land, if that person knows or has reasonable cause to believe the other is so entitled.[5]

Signed: [by or on behalf of the Building Owner]

Dated:

Notes

1 This notice is an essential preliminary to exercising rights of entry for workmen (s 8(3)) or surveyors (s 8(6)). It must be served by the building owner.
2 The adjoining owner can be served by addressing him as 'the owner' and, if necessary, fixing the notice to the premises (s 15(2)).
3 Occupiers must also be served. For methods of service see s 15(1).
4 14 days is the normal minimum. In emergencies, such notice must be given as is reasonably practicable (s 8(3)(a) and (6)(a)).
5 This Precedent is designed to give enough explanation of the parties' rights of entry to pave the way for criminal sanctions under s 16. Clause 2 could be omitted if this is not thought necessary.

8.   Formal Request[1]

Party Wall etc Act 1996 ('the 1996 Act')

Re Notice[2] dated from [Name of Building Owner]
to [Name of Adjoining Owner]

To: [Name of appropriate Owner or Surveyor]

of   [Address]

THIS is a formal request under section 10(4)(b) [10(7)] [10(8)] of the 1996 Act made for the purpose of determining the dispute arising from the above-mentioned Notice.

I HEREBY REQUEST

8.1   [If under section 10(4)(b)][3]
that you appoint a Surveyor under section 10(1)(b) of the 1996 Act.
If you fail to make an appointment in writing within 10 days of the service of this request on you, I shall be entitled to make an appointment on your behalf.

8.2   [If under section 10(7)][4]
that you act effectively in the dispute by [eg agreeing with me [my Surveyor] a timetable for determining the said dispute and proceeding in accordance with the timetable]. If you fail to do so within 10 days of the service of this request on you, I [my Surveyor] will be entitled to proceed ex parte to take those steps.

8.3   [If under section 10(8)][5]
that [in view of the [refusal to act/death/etc] of Mr   the third Surveyor] you concur with me, in selecting a third Surveyor [in his place] under section 10(1)(b) [10(9)] of the 1996 Act. I set out below the names of 3 persons whom I would approve for the purpose. If you do not approve any of them I further request that you notify me of the names of 3 persons whom you would approve. If you fail to accede to this request in writing within 10 days of its service on you, I shall be entitled to apply to the Appointing Officer [Secretary of State] to make the selection.

[List 3 names]

Signed: [by the appropriate Owner or Surveyor]

Dated:

Notes

1 Requests of this kind can readily be incorporated in a letter, provided it is written by, and served on, the appropriate person. They all have to be 'served', and must therefore be in writing. (Contrast s 10(11) where it is sufficient merely to 'call upon' the third surveyor, a process so informal that no Precedent is offered.)

2 This will be the initiating notice served by the building owner under ss 1(2), (5), 3(1) or 6(5).

3 Under this section the request must be made by or on behalf of the aggrieved owner, and served on the defaulting owner.

4 Under this section the request must be by the aggrieved owner or his surveyor, and served on the defaulting surveyor. It is the surveyor who becomes entitled to proceed ex parte, so that the request comes better from him. The alternative references to 'my surveyor' are appropriate only if the owner makes the request.

5 Under this section the request must be made by the aggrieved surveyor, and served on the defaulting surveyor. The request may arise under s 10(1)(b) (failure to select) or s 10(9) (refusal etc of third Surveyor). It is prudent to offer a choice of three names.

9.   Appointment of Surveyors[1]

Party Wall etc Act 1996 ('the 1996 Act')

Re Notice[2] dated   from [Name of Building Owner]
to [Name of Adjoining Owner]

9.1   Pursuant to section 10(1)(b) of the 1996 Act I [Name of Owner] hereby appoint Mr   of
to act as my Surveyor for the purposes of the dispute arising from the above-mentioned notice.

9.2   Pursuant to section 10(1)(a) of the 1996 Act, I [Name of Owner] hereby concur in the appointment of Mr   of
to act as the agreed Surveyor for the purposes [etc as above].

9.3   Pursuant to section 10(4) of the 1996 Act, I [Name of Owner] hereby appoint Mr   of
to act as the Surveyor of [Name of other Owner] (who has refused [neglected] to make an appointment on his own behalf) for the purposes [etc as above].

9.4   Pursuant to section 10(5) of the 1996 Act, I [Name of Owner] hereby appoint Mr   of
to act as my Surveyor for the purposes [etc as above] in place of Mr who has [deemed himself incapable of acting].

Notes

1   These are the four forms of appointment provided for by s 10. In each case the appointment should be signed by the appropriate owner.

2   This will be the initiating notice served by the building owner under ss 1(2), (5), 3(1) or 6(5).

10. Selection of Third Surveyor[1]

Party Wall etc Act 1996 ('the 1996 Act')

Re Notice[2] dated   from [Name of Building Owner]
to [Name of Adjoining Owner]

10.1   Pursuant to section 10(1)(b) of the 1996 Act we, [Name], the Surveyor appointed by the Building Owner, and [Name], the Surveyor appointed by the Adjoining Owner, hereby select Mr   of
to act as the third Surveyor for the purposes of the dispute arising from the above-mentioned notice.

10.2   Pursuant to section 10(8) of the 1996 Act, I [Name of appointing officer], being the officer appointed for the purpose by the
Council, whose area includes the properties described in the above-mentioned notice, hereby select Mr   of
to act as the third Surveyor [etc as above].

10.3   Pursuant to section 10(9) of the 1996 Act we [Names], (the Surveyors appointed by the Building Owner and the Adjoining Owner respectively) hereby select Mr   of
to act as the third Surveyor [etc as above] in the place of [Name], who [died on the   ].

Notes

1 These are the three forms of selection of the third surveyor provided for by s 10. Under s 10(8) the selection must be made, and signed, either by the appointing officer (see s 20) or the Secretary of State. The other two selections must be made and signed by each of the parties' surveyors.

2 This will be the initiating notice served by the building owner under ss 1(2), (5), 3(1) or 6(5).

11. AWARD[1]

Party Wall etc Act 1996 ('the 1996 Act')

WHEREAS   of
('the Building Owner') the owner of the premises known as
on the [date] served upon   of
('the Adjoining Owner') the owner of the adjoining premises known as
                notice under section [1(2)/1(5)/3(1)/6(5)] of the 1996 Act
of his intention to execute works described therein

AND WHEREAS a dispute has arisen between the Building Owner and the
Adjoining Owner ('the Parties')

AND WHEREAS the Adjoining Owner has appointed
of

to act as his Surveyor and the Building Owner has appointed
of

to act as his Surveyor ('the Parties' Surveyors')

AND WHEREAS the Parties' Surveyors have selected
of

to act as Third Surveyor in accordance with the provisions of the 1996 Act.

NOW WE, the Parties' Surveyors, being two of the three Surveyors so
appointed, having inspected the said premises, DO HEREBY AWARD AND
DETERMINE as follows:

1.   We find the following facts:
       [(a) That the wall separating   and   is a party [fence] wall
            within the meaning of the Act.
        (b) That the said wall, although old, is sufficient for the needs of the
            Adjoining Owner.
        (c) That the condition of the said wall is as described in the Schedule of
            Condition dated   attached hereto and forming
            part of this Award.
       etc].

2.   Fourteen days after the service of this Award on him the Building Owner shall be at liberty, but without obligation, to carry out the following works ('the Works'):

[List them]

3.   No material deviation from the Works shall be made without the prior agreement of the Surveyor appointed by the Adjoining Owner.

4.   The Building Owner shall:
   (a) Execute the whole of the Works at the sole cost of the Building Owner.
   (b) Take all reasonable precautions and provide all necessary shoring to retain the Adjoining Owner's land and buildings.
   (c) Make good all structural or decorative damage to the adjoining building occasioned by the Works in materials to match the existing works.
   (d) Hold the Adjoining Owner free from liability in respect of any injury or loss of life to any person or damage to property caused by or in consequence of the execution of the Works and the costs of making any justified claims.
   (e) Permit the Adjoining Owner's Surveyor to have access to the Building Owner's premises at all reasonable times during the progress of the Works.
   (f) Carry out the whole of the Works, so far as practicable, from the Building Owner's side. Where access to the Adjoining Owner's premises adjacent to the party wall is required, reasonable notice shall be given. Any scaffolding or screens will be removed as soon as possible and dust and debris cleared away from time to time as necessary.
   (g) Have the right to enter the property of the Adjoining Owner between the hours of 9.00 am and 5.30 pm, Mondays to Fridays, excluding Public Holidays, for the purpose of carrying out the following works:

[List works requiring entry on adjoining land]

5.   The Building Owner's Surveyor shall be permitted access to the Adjoining Owner's property from time to time during the progress of the works at reasonable times and after giving reasonable notice.

6.   The whole of the Works shall be executed in accordance with Building Regulations and statutory requirements (including the requirements of the Control of Pollution Act 1974, the Environmental Protection Act 1990, the Health and Safety at Work etc Act 1974) and the requirements of any authority having jurisdiction over the Works, (including the Local

Authorities in whose area the work is being carried out, the Health and Safety Inspectorate and HM Inspectorate of Pollution) and to the satisfaction of the Building Control Officer or independent Certifying Officer and shall be executed in a proper and workmanlike manner in sound and suitable materials in accordance with the terms of this Award to the reasonable satisfaction of the adjoining Owner's Surveyor.

7.   The Works shall be carried through with reasonable expedition after commencement and so as to avoid any unnecessary inconvenience to the Adjoining Owner and adjoining occupiers.

8.   The two signed copies of the Award shall be served forthwith on the Parties by their respective Surveyors.

9.   The Building Owner shall pay the fees of the Surveyor appointed by the Adjoining Owner (to be advised) plus VAT, in connection with the settling and carrying into effect of this Award.

10. The Parties' Surveyors reserve the right to make and issue one or more further Awards as may be necessary. If they cannot agree, the dispute shall be determined as provided in the 1996 Act.

11. This Award shall be null and void if the Works do not commence within twelve months from the date of service of this Award on the Building Owner.

12. Save so far as is necessary for the execution of the Works, nothing in this Award shall be construed as prejudicially affecting any right of light or air or any other easement whatever.

Signed: [by the Parties' Surveyors]

Dated:

Note

1   This Precedent is adapted from an award kindly provided by Mr A Schatunowski, FRICS. Its provisions are typical, but by way of example only.

12.   Notice Requiring Security[1]

Party Wall etc Act 1996 ('the 1996 Act')

Re Notice dated   from [Name of Building Owner]
            to [Name of Adjoining Owner]

To: [Name of Appropriate Owner]

of [Address]

THIS is a notice under section 12(1) [12(2)] of the 1996 Act requiring you to
give security in respect of works described in the above-mentioned notice.

I HEREBY GIVE YOU NOTICE that:

12.1   [If the notice is under section 12(1)][2]

I require you to give security in respect of the said works, by [providing a bond
in the sum of £   ], or in such other sum or manner as may be agreed
between us or determined by the Surveyors under section 10 of the 1996 Act.

12.2   [If the notice is under section 12(2)][3]

1.   I require you to give security for the expenses which will fall to be
         defrayed by you, by [depositing the sum of £   in a joint account
         in the names of the Solicitors acting for each of us], or in such other sum
         or manner as may be agreed between us or determined by the Surveyors
         under section 10 of the 1996 Act.

2.   If you fail to give security within one month of the date of service of this
         notice on you, or of determination by the Surveyors, the notice which
         you served on me under section 12(1) of the 1996 Act will cease to have
         effect.

Signed: [by or on behalf of the Appropriate Owner]

Dated:

Notes

1 See s 12(1) (by adjoining owner) and s 12(2) (by building owner). These notices must both
  be served before the building owner starts work.

2 There are always likely to be expenses for which the adjoining owner would like security, for example in case the building owner leaves the work uncompleted.

3 Although s 12(2)(b) entitles the building owner to require security merely because the adjoining owner has done so, it is thought that security could only be awarded in respect of expenses which the Act imposes on the adjoining owner.

13. Appeal to county court

IN THE   COUNTY COURT   No. of Matter:

IN THE MATTER of the Party Wall etc Act 1996[1]

and

IN THE MATTER of an Award dated

BETWEEN   [Name of appealing Owner]   Appellant
                     and
             [Name of other Owner]   Respondent

To the District Judge of the   County Court.[2]

The Appellant desires to appeal against the Award of [Name of Surveyors who made the Award] ('the Surveyors') made on [date], of which a copy is attached hereto.[3]

The grounds of the appeal are as follows:

[Set out grounds of law or fact,[4] for example:

1.   The Surveyors had no jurisdiction to order the works to be executed, because they do not fall within any paragraph of section 2(2) of the 1996 Act.

2.   The Surveyors were wrong in law to order any part of the expense to be borne by the Appellant.

3.   The Surveyors erred in finding as a fact that:

       [Set out findings attacked]

4.   The said findings were against the weight of the evidence.

etc].

[*cont*]

We request you to enter this appeal for hearing in the   County Court
[and to direct that the return day shall be a day fixed for a pre-trial review[5]].

The name and address of the Respondent is

The Appellant's address for service is

Dated:

Signed:

(Solicitors for the Appellant)

Notes

1 Under s 10(17) this appeal must be filed with the county court within 14 days of service of the award on the appellant. It is made under County Court Rules 1981, Ord 3, r 6. This Precedent is an adaptation of County Court Practice Form N209.

2 The appropriate venue is the court for the district in which the award was made or given (see CCR 1981, Ord 4, r 9).

3 A copy of the award must be filed at the same time (see CCR 1981, Ord 6, r 2).

4 The appeal is a rehearing (see para **10.2**), so that grounds of law or fact can be relied on.

5 A pre-trial review can be directed (see CCR 1981, Ord 6, r 5), and in view of the scope of an appeal, this will often be advisable.

14. Account[1]

Party Wall etc Act 1996 ('the 1996 Act')

Re Award dated[2]

To: [Name of Adjoining Owner]

of   [Address]

From: [Name of Building Owner]

of   [Address]

THIS account is served on you under section 13(1) of the 1996 Act and has been prepared in accordance with that section to show the expenses payable by you under the terms of the above-mentioned Award.

Kindly take note as follows:

1.   I require you to pay to me the sum of £   shown in the account to be payable by you.

2.   (a) If within one month of the service of this account on you, you serve on me a notice stating objections to the account, a dispute will be deemed to arise between us, which must be determined by the Surveyors.[3]
        (b) If not, you will be deemed to have no objection to the account, and must pay me the said sum.[4]

3.   Until you pay the sum due, the property in the works executed pursuant to the said Award will be vested solely in me.[5]

Signed: [by or on behalf of Building Owner]

Dated:

Notes

1 See s 13(1). The account must be served within 2 months from the completion of the works (see para **11.7**).

2 The adjoining owner's liability for expenses will normally arise from an award.

3 See s 13(2).

4 See s 13(3).

5 See s 14(2) and para **11.8**.

15.   Notice of Objections to Account[1]

Party Wall etc Act 1996 ('the 1996 Act')

To: [Name of Building Owner]

of   [Address]

From: [Name of Adjoining Owner]

of   [Address]

THIS notice is served on you under section 13(2) of the 1996 Act, in response to the account served by you on [me].

I GIVE YOU NOTICE that I object to the said account on the following grounds:

[1.   The particulars of the expenses and work are insufficient.

2.   No deduction is made [in respect of item   ] for old materials.

3.   The work and materials [in respect of items   ] are valued at excessive rates and prices.

etc].

Signed: [by or on behalf of Adjoining Owner]

Dated:

Appendix 5

THE PARTY WALL ETC BILL IN PARLIAMENT

The Bill was introduced as a Private Members Bill into the House of Lords by the Earl of Lytton, himself a chartered surveyor in private practice. In the House of Commons it was sponsored by Sir Sydney Chapman MP. Although the Bill was a Private Members Bill, it received Government support.

The relevant references in Hansard are as follows.

House of Lords
(1) House of Lords Debates 95/96, Vol 568, 31 January 1996, Col 1535 (second reading).

(2) House of Lords Debates 95/96, Vol 572, 22 May 1996, Col 931 (Committee).

(3) House of Lords Debates 95/96, Vol 572, 4 June 1996, Col 1160 (report received).

(4) House of Lords Debates 95/96, Vol 972, 11 June 1996, Col 1575 (third reading).

House of Commons
House of Commons Debates 95/96, Vol 281, 12 July 1996, Col 760 (second reading, Committee stage, report stage, third reading, Royal Assent).

The proceedings in the House of Commons were purely formal, the Act completing its passage in one day without objection (despite a strongly worded Parliamentary Briefing from The Law Society opposing the Bill). In the House of Lords, the report of second reading and Committee stage (references given above) should be consulted.

INDEX

References in the right-hand column are to paragraph numbers or Appendix number.